The Journal of Practice Teaching & Learning

Social Work • Health • Nursing

Volume Seven, Number Two, 2006-07

Contents

Editorial
3

We all love playing in the sand!
Using sand play therapy in critical reflection with students
in practice placement
Debbie Amas
6

Social work practice with Arab Muslim women living in Western societies
Bassima Schbley and Mark Kaufman
25

Failing to fail students
in the caring professions:
Is the assessment process failing the professions?
Mike Shapton
39

Human geography and questions for social work education
Pat Wilkinson and Gavin Bissell
55

Notes for contributors
69

MANAGING EDITOR
Lynda Deacon, Social Work Consultant

EDITOR
Steve Ambler, Independent Practice Teacher and Lecturer. Formerly Practice Learning Coordinator, Anglia Ruskin University

BOOK REVIEWS EDITOR
Adrian Black Principal Lecturer in Social Work, Anglia Ruskin University

CORRESPONDING EDITORS
Annette Bolin Lecturer in Social Work, University West, Trollhattan (Sweden)
Lesley Cooper Dean, Lyle S. Hallman Faculty of Social Work, Wilfred Laurier University (Canada)
Greta Galloway Academic Advisor and Senior Lecturer, Dept of Social Work and Community Welfare, James Cook University, Cairns (Australia)
Professor Donna Love Dept of Social Work, Washburn University, Topeka (N America)
Hanna Nel Dept of Social Work, University of Johannesburg (Republic of South Afrsica)

EDITORIAL BOARD
Mary Anderson Lecturer and Practice Advisor, School of Community Science, University of Ulster
Jennifer Bernard Director of Product Management, City & Guilds
Lesley Best Head of Social Work, University College Northampton
Professor Fred Besthorn University of Iowa, Cedar Falls
Professor Jan Fook Professor of Social Work, Southampton University
Professor Mark Doel Research Professor of Social Work, Sheffield Hallam University
Graham Ixer Head of Social Work Education, General Social Care Council
Professor Tony Leiba Mental Health Studies, Faculty of Health and Social Care, South Bank University
Helena Low Development Manager, CAIPE, London
Professor Jonathan Parker Professor of Social Work, Bournemouth University
Bob Sapey Senior Lecturer, Dept of Applied Social Science, Cartmel College, Lancaster University
Cathy Tyler, Practice Teacher, Northumbria
Janice West Lecturer in Social Work, Glasgow Caledonian University
Colin Whittington Whittington Research and Development, Bromley

SUBMISSIONS
Papers should be submitted to Steve Ambler, Editor, *Journal of Practice Teaching in Health and Social Work*, 7 Ermine Crescent, Stilton, Peterborough PE7 3RD. steve@amblernet.com.

BOOKS FOR REVIEW
Books and other materials for review should be sent to the Editor at the above address.

OTHER CORRESPONDENCE
All other correspondence regarding the Journal should be made to the publishers, Whiting & Birch Ltd., 90 Dartmouth Road, Forest Hill, London, SE23 3HZ, England. Tel 020 8244 2421. Fax 020 8244 2448.

SUBSCRIPTION RATES

	UK/Europe	N America	Elsewhere
Libraries	£155.00	US$250.00	£165.00
Organisations	£75.00	US$120.00	£85.00
Individuals	£35.00	US$65.00	£40.00

Subscriptions are accepted and entered for whole volumes only. Payment may be made by sterling cheque drawn on UK bank, US dollar cheque, international money order in sterling or credit card (Mastercard, Visa). Subscription enquiries should be addressed to the publishers.

CLAIMS
Claims must be made within eight weeks of publication of the subsequent issue.

ADVERTISING
Current rates and specifications may be obtained from the publisher.

© Whiting and Birch. All rights reserved; no part of this publication may be reproduced without prior consent from the publisher.

ISSNs 1460-6690 (print) / 1746-6105 (online). EAN for single issue 9781861775009

Printed in England and the United States by Lightning Source

The views expressed in articles in this journal are those of the authors and do not necessarily reflect those of the Editorial Board or the authors' agencies.

Editorial

One of the most enjoyable aspects of attending last years Sixth International Conference on Practice Teaching and Field Education in York was being able to meet colleagues from over twelve different countries. During the conference a meeting was held to explore the possibility of developing an international organisation for practice learning and teaching. The proposed objectives of the organisation are:

1. To disseminate good practice in field education/practice learning on a global basis.
2. To build and maintain an international network of appropriate knowledge and expertise.
3. To create an international community of learning in all aspects of field/practice learning in social work and health.

If you would like to participate in the proposed organisation please contact me, my contact details are on page 2 of this issue.

The Seventh Conference will take place from Monday 7th to Wednesday 9th July 2008, again in York. The theme will be; Having Faith in Practice Learning: exploring the importance of faith, spirituality and religion in practice learning / field education.

*

This issue starts with a creative article by Debbie Amas who has developed the therapeutic technique of Sand Play Therapy with social work students as a learning tool. Her paper describes a process of learning by facilitating a group seminar with BA in Social Work students who undertook a sand tray exercise. The students were able to explore practice issues and enhance the important skills of critical reflection and linking 'taught' theory-to-practice.

Bassima Schbley and Mark Kaufman, both social work educators from the United States contend that social work learning should not be insulated from the influences of religious beliefs and practices. Their article discusses the results of a small-scale survey of Arab Muslim women living in the USA and offers suggestions on how practice teachers can use their findings (and that of others) to enhance the cultural competence of social work students.

Mike Shapton's paper addresses the difficulties encountered when students are 'failing'. From his personal perspective he argues that on occasions professionals will 'fail to fail' due to the complexity of the issues and tasks involved. He suggests strategies that concentrate on systems and organisational responses rather than solely focussing on those professionals who assess competence to practice.

Human geography and its relevance to the core social work value of social responsibility is the subject of Pat Wilkinson and Gavin Bissell's innovative paper. They argue that since the demise of community social work (in the 1980s) the profession has perhaps ignored the importance of the physical environment and its relationship to effective practice. They also suggest that the student's campus experience can be used to foster social responsibilty.

Steve Ambler

The 7th International Conference *for* Practice Learning and Field Education in Health and Social Work

Having faith in practice learning:
exploring the importance of faith, spirituality and religion in practice learning and field education

Monday 7th - Wednesday 9th July 2008
St John's University College, York

This year, the conference will examine the complexities of teaching and learning in increasingly multi-faith communities, while identifying and maintaining our professional values, tasks and boundaries.

The conference will be of interest to people working in practice and education within social work, nursing, counselling, mental health, public health, local and regional government, social care, and community regeneration.

**More details of the programme will be posted as they become available at:
http://www.whitingbirch.net/ip005.shtml**

We all love playing in the sand! Using sand play therapy in critical reflection with students in practice placement

Debbie Amas[1]

Summary: This paper introduces a creative therapeutic technique used in Projective Play Therapy called sand play therapy that I evolved in my work with students on placement to help them reflect on practice. In this paper I describe my experience of facilitating a sand tray exercise I devised as part of a group seminar programme for BA Social Work students to help them both explore their practice in placement and examine Learning Outcomes linked with knowledge from their module learning. Finally I discuss the evaluation undertaken with participating students about the usefulness of the exercise as an intuitive reflective tool.

Keywords:sand play; projective play therapy; practice learning; social work; critical reflection

1. Tutor. Anglia Ruskin University / independent practice teacher/trainer

Address for Correspondence:, Faculty of Health and Social Care, Anglia Ruskin University, The Webb Building, East Road, Cambridge, CB1 1PT.
D.A.Amas@anglia.ac.uk

Introduction

I was first introduced to the sand play technique in the mid nineties when I worked as a team leader of social workers carrying out Direct Work and Life Story work with children and young people. Our team were fortunate to have a qualified social worker who was also a trained art therapist. He taught us how sand play could be used therapeutically with children and young people in a Direct Work setting by facilitating a direct experience of the technique for our team. We were intrigued as our colleague took each one of us through what he called a projective play exercise. The work, or play, happened in a wooden box full of play sand surrounded by amazing small toys, objects, jewels, candles and jugs of water. One by one he encouraged us to build a landscape representing our world and to explore it narratively with each other. On that day our colleague introduced us to a powerful and flexible therapeutic tool which we later came to use to reflect on dynamics and power relationships during difficulties within our team and in the wider organisation. At the time I was also a Practice Teacher and had a student for whom the sand play technique became a useful tool that helped her to construct an understanding of power relationships and team dynamics in a tangible way in the sand tray. Since that time I am always prompted to use the sand tray exercise in my practice with individual student/practitioners. In the two seminars where I conducted the sand play technique I found that it can be a powerful and thoughtful group work tool that provokes deep learning, particularly in considering anti oppressive/ anti discriminatory practice, ethics and values and use/ abuse/ misuse of power.

Deep learning processes are essential for students if they are to develop critically reflective practice acknowledged as an essential pre requisite for practicing safely with service users:

> ... because of the responsibilities that social workers and probations officers carry, and the influence and impact they can have on the lives of vulnerable people, that as well as being skilled and knowledgeable that they treat people with respect and are honest, trustworthy and reliable. They must be self aware and critically reflective and their practice must be founded on, informed by and capable, of being judged against a clear value base. (General Social Care Council, 2006, p.6)

The development of reflective practice in Higher Education mainly influenced by Donald A. Schon throughout the 1970s and 1980s has led to a number of taught techniques that help students critically reflect in spaces where practice and knowledge meet (Kolb, 1984; Gibbs, 1985). The space may be facilitated in practice tutorials, seminars, small group teaching, as well as in consultation and mentoring. Models of small group teaching and one to one tutorials with focussed exercises allow opportunities for students to practice reflexivity that takes them out of routine learning with the inherent intention of identifying and deepening knowledge. Thus students should become explicit parties to a contextualised course design that embeds opportunities for breadth in learning. (Brockbank and McGill, 2000).

In the social work degree students need to reflect not only on cultural, organisational, socio-political, procedural and governmental frameworks and theoretical contexts of their work, but also on personal values, all of which impact on the lives of people who use the services where they undertake their Practice Learning Opportunities. Students need to develop confidence as practitioners if they are to develop skills that allow them to challenge, advocate, work in partnership with and collaborate across professions in complex circumstances in the best interests of service users.

In developing the sand tray technique to work with student/ practitioners my aim is to bring the material world of practice to a learning space in a unique way, giving students a powerful opportunity to reflect on a landscape they make intuitively about their practice in a sand play exercise. My vision in developing the idea is to use creative practice in reflection in order to more deeply ground their knowledge.

Inevitably there has been some discussion about the conditions needed so that critical reflection can inspire confidence in social work practice. In reflecting, students are asked to consider uncomfortable aspects of their work which may provoke anxiety for a variety of reasons. Firstly the practitioner/student is aware that practice is governed by a framework of competence within a driver of performance management and social work modernisation that can act as a barrier, or as Baldwin (2004) states, 'threat' to critical reflection. Secondly, student/practitioners may unconsciously, or consciously, reframe practice narratives for a knowing audience within a framework of professional understanding or cultural 'fit', possibly seeing the scrutiny of practice as a personal criticism of their work. (Taylor, 2006). Yipp (2005) identifies processes in critical reflection that by their nature will relate to psycho-dynamic theories in the examination of relationships, including transference and counter-transference. Further, practice may be examined in an atmosphere of comparative analysis where the practitioner measures or compares their performance with others:

> That means that the individual social worker is evaluating not only his or her performance but also his or her personality, professional competence and identity. (Yip, 2006, p.780).

Clearly, the student/practitioner is vulnerable within the critically reflective process. Care is needed to ensure that the conditions set up to examine practice increases self determination and instils robust professionalism. The projective play process facilitated in the sand tray exercise, providing it is set up correctly, is a creative space for the student/practitioner to explore practice. The factors that threaten good reflective practice remain present and need to be acknowledged within the context of the exercise. That is, the exercise cannot take away the power of assessment, management frameworks, possible personal anxiety and oppression in working environments. What it offers is a creative and potentially powerful way of examining what is going on. The making of the sand landscape helps student/practitioners construct an understanding and potentially resolve issues or find a deeper meanings and contexts for their work. The following brief history of projective play therapy which includes sand tray therapy, demonstrates how the technique is removed from traditional interpretive or psychoanalytic perspectives towards a solution focussed model. This not only models good practice for student/practitioners, but provides them with an empowerment tool that can be used in Direct Work.

History of projective play processes and sand play therapy

Sand play therapy was developed by Margaret Lowenfeld who began her pioneering work in what she termed 'projective play therapies' with children as early as 1937 when she realised that childs play was not an accident but as an essential function of childhood basically concerned with the adaptive process ... continues throughout life ... and affects man's ability to survive in his physical universe ... and social environments. (1967, p.2)

The unique feature of Lowenfeld's therapy with children was the value base in the child's exploration of their own world without using psychotherapeutic interpretation in a conventional sense. Her view was that the worlds she facilitated in the creation of landscapes in sand trays, and other play therapeutic techniques she developed, belonged wholly to the child who could explore that world within a safe and trusting relationship with an adult in any way they wished, much as they would in natural play:

> The primary attribute of the therapist was that he/she was a trustworthy, child friendly adult who was genuinely interested in providing the child with the means to express and to understand him/herself. Thus, in sand play she helped children enter and explore their Worlds. She felt that the World, not the interpretive therapist, needed to confront its maker. In fact, when she asked children to introduce their Worlds and their characters to her, she validated their capacity to create, to experience, and to revise their own meanings. Whenever she honoured the child as the keeper of the story-of-meaning, she learned to speak the language of the child rather than expecting the child to speak the language of the therapist. (De Domenico, 2002)

The sand tray exercise was one of many techniques developed by Lowenfeld in what she termed projective play therapy to encourage children to explore themselves and their world through play with the intention of facilitating potential solutions, or moving through issues that impacted on their lives, such as loss, change, trauma and bereavement. The ongoing development of play therapy through to current times has demonstrated the importance of observing play and finding ways to open up a space for children that is therapeutic, safe, engaging and fun, but that also helps them to think about their own solutions to situations they decide how to define and narrate for themselves.

Lowenfeld mainly considered her work as a tool for children and young people. However, projective play techniques were soon recognised as a tool that could be used with adults. Jungian and Gestalt therapists saw the potential of the sand tray technique for bringing unconscious material into the conscious world (Stevens 2004). Like many play and creative arts therapy tools sand play has gone on to prove itself. It can work effectively with those who have faced deep traumas, such as war, disaster and terrorism with children and adults. In my view, within a broad spectrum of people who use services from individuals, families and groups and within a consultation or supervision processes for health and social care professionals, the sand tray technique offers an opportunity for anyone explore their world with new eyes.

Using the sand tray exercise

Before commencing with my description of the exercise I used with my BA Social Work Seminar Groups I would like to emphasise the experiential nature of the tool and the importance of working with the sand tray prior to using it with others. Where the Practice Teacher is part of the organisation providing the Practice Learning Opportunity particular care will be needed in considering some of the issues surrounding the safety of critical reflection already discussed. At the beginning of this article I described how a team member trained in therapeutic arts facilitated an experience of a sand tray exercise. I find working intimately with the sand tray to be a very powerful learning within itself, acquainting me not only with its strength as a cathartic and solution focussed tool, but also to the very sound principles of a non interpretive approach:

> Sand play evokes very deep realities. It cuts across many familial and cultural taboos as it activates the deep, primordial integrative forces of the psyche. Whether an educator, a trained expressive, ar or play therapist or whether an accomplished verbal, behavioural, or cognitive clinician, each sand play facilitator needs to use the sand tray for his/her own personal growth and development before integrating the tool into the play- and consultation room.' (De Domenico, 1995)

Another crucial element in introducing the technique is to acknowledge that it is a therapeutic tool. The use of any therapeutic model or practice must be 'held' in a safe space for participants. The experience will be far more engaging and useful if the participants don't feel they are being blamed, tested or validated. The Tutor/Practice Teacher relationship with the student/practitioner is a powerful dynamic that needs to be acknowledged within the context of the exercise. I have found that students are open to exploring their work, but are also cautious because they know their values and issues may be challenging as well as challenged. Our occupation demands standards and codes of practice that ensure open and transparent communication. Such standards and codes expose practitioners and students across the profession to face potentially difficult moral and ethical dilemmas. The sand tray adds a dimension to reflective space that should be experienced first hand by a facilitator to help them understand the powerful dynamic that is being introduced to the reflective process.

For the purpose of preparing for the exercise I would advise that the facilitator find a trusted colleague, mentor or supervisor and work together until there is a feeling of intimate acquaintance with the sand tray. A discussion about the feelings evoked is a useful way to analyse processes. For instance, was there a temptation as a facilitator to interpret the landscape? As a person building the landscape what was it like to see it emerging? Was there anything surprising or unexpected? What would help the environment to feel comfortable? This should inspire ideas to develop a careful lesson plan. It seems to me that this expressive tool is flexible enough to be developed in many directions. I found that utilising reflection 'in' action and critically reflecting 'on' sessions using reflection models in adult education has been helpful for me in developing the sand play exercise in the class room (Schon 1987). I used Gibbs (1988) reflective cycle to analyse the group sessions I ran. The first session I facilitated was an observed teaching session as part of my Post-Graduate Certificate in Higher Education. I was able to reflect on the exercise with the observing tutor as well as receive feedback from the students. As a result of running the second session, reflection gained from student evaluation and feedback led to further adjustments in planning future sessions. I learned a great deal about the added group work dynamic that is helping me with future action and planning. I have also reflected considerably on how the exercise links into the knowledge and theory base of practice so that I can help students unpack what is going on in their landscape.

The following description of my work with the sand tray is by no means definitive and anyone considering facilitating a session should consider undertaking further research, training and experience before practicing it with students.

The sand tray and equipment

The original sand tray methodology advises very specific measurements for a wooden box that is painted blue at the bottom. Because I am travelling with the equipment I have to improvise and use plastic gravel trays that I purchased from a local garden centre. The boxes must be water tight, quite sturdy and big enough to allow students to swirl water around and make a good sized landscape. My sand trays are 40cm x 20cm with a depth of 5cms. It is useful to look on the sand tray/ World Play web site where different shapes and sizes of sand trays are pictured. I provided water and play sand. I also brought a large bag of small objects, such as toy cars, small doll house dolls, worry dolls (purchased from Oxfam), toy animals, ethnic beads, small candles, old jewellery, interesting little boxes, some of which contained small mirrors, crystals, twigs, pine cones, ribbons and any other objects I think are interesting and could be used. I am always on the look out for small objects of interest and often find things at car boot sales, markets and in my children's bedrooms!! I also have a number of small houseplant shovels and forks that can be used for scoring interesting patterns in the sand which can also be moulded with fingers and hands when damp. I spread the toys and objects out on a separate table to allow students to choose easily. Each landscape can be photographed so that students have a record of their work. A digital camera may be used and the pictures then emailed to individual students following the sessions. Students can also take their own photos using mobile phones or their own cameras.

The space

A space needs to be set up that is comfortable and secure where no disturbances will occur. The group exercise is done in two's, and I have found the best way to do this is to set up a small table with a sand tray in the middle and a chair either side. For practical reasons the sand is already piled up in the tray ready to use and several jugs of water are available. Small tables for two are set up around the room arranged so that there is as little interference of each others narratives as possible.

At the beginning of the session I have a semicircle of chairs where the group sit together so that I can introduce the exercise. When the pairings have been made the students can take their chairs to a table with a sand tray on it to begin the exercise. I pay attention to the ambience of the room, perhaps providing quiet music when students arrive, having some cushions, incense, burning oil or scented candles, if this is acceptable within fire and safety regulations. I find it helps to give students a sense of arrival in an atmosphere of calm.

Setting up the exercise

Students must know about the exercise in advance. In the cases I am describing I explained the exercise during the introductory seminar at the beginning of term and ensured the students knew date on which it would be facilitated. In introducing the exercise I explained some of the theoretical aspects of the sand tray technique and also provided some references on critical reflection and Direct Work/ Projective Play Therapy on a handout. I also explored how the technique might help in considering learning outcomes and facilitated a discussion around the acknowledgement of power relationships. I explained important logistical information, such as not arriving late or disturbing the session in any way. The session requires a commitment on the part of the student to ensure everyone has a good experience.

The main issues I have explored in sessions of sand tray work with students in placement are power and the misuse of power, anti discriminatory/ oppressive practice and empowering practice. The Learning Outcomes for the session were made explicitly to the students on a work sheet:

- Evaluate your practice using a creative visualisation tool
- Analyse your practice within the contexts of Learning Outcomes in your stage 1 placement
- Develop ideas for using creative social work tools in direct work with service users in your practice

On the day of the session the exercise was already set up when the students came into the room. It is essential that there are no disturbances so I ensured that mobile phones were switched off. During the session students must realise that even though they are working in pairs they are part of the supportive process for the whole group and need to respect others by engaging in their own process quietly and not creating a distraction for others. At the beginning of the session I asked students to make an agreement to work with each other respectfully. The ground rules we worked with in the session I am describing were as follows:

- Respect confidentiality
- Keep the exercise quiet and try to absorb yourself in it
- Do not chat, or get chatty
- Practice listening skills
- Support each other and stay safe

I asked the students to sit comfortably on their chair in the semi circle with their back supported and both feet on the floor, and to close their eyes. I asked them to breathe naturally and allow the out breath to relax muscles and tensions. My intention in doing this was to help the students have a sense that they are beginning a process that requires their full attention and focus. Pairs can be picked by students choosing partners themselves or by putting numbers into a bowl and pairing those with the same numbers. The pairs then go and sit at a table with a sand tray opposite each other. I asked students to decide between them who will build their landscape first and who will act as the facilitator. Each student had a work sheet containing instructions for carrying out the exercise.

Carrying out the exercise

The student facilitator asks the student opposite them to close their eyes and to think about a case that they have been working on, a scenario that has interested them within their placement, or a dynamic they would like to explore. The student facilitator then takes the student they are working with through a guided visualisation instructed in the following way on their work sheet:

'Visualise a case or situation that you are working with in your placement, one that is causing you to reflect, or that is making you feel uncomfortable, or raising issues for you.

(Ask the partner, 'Have you chosen a case?' – allow them to nod. Don't continue till they have a case. If they can't think of a case then encourage them to think about a situation that is happening in the placement. Be flexible – encourage them to think of any situation in their placement that interests them)

Once they have settled on a scenario continue with something like the following – adapt what you are saying to support your partner's thoughts:

'Soon I am going to ask you to build a picture of your thoughts in the sand. First, I would like you to think about everything that is happening in the case/situation you are thinking of. See the service user in your mind. See all the others involved, other people and agencies. Think about how they all interact and work with this case/situation. What are the relationships between everyone? Where are you in the case? Are there any aspects that remind you of people in your own life? Do any of the people or organisations conjure up pictures of animals or objects? Start to build a scene or landscape in your mind. Imagine the case in colours, in animals, in landscapes, as if in a dream – what would it look like?

Leave a little silence then ask your partner to open their eyes and build a picture of their scene in the sand.

They can manipulate the sand and use the items on the table. You can sit with them in silence and watch as they build the picture. Make mental notes of how you feel being the listener and observer.
When the sand tray picture is complete ask your partner to explain it to you. Make some rough written notes together of your findings and feelings.

Look at the Learning Outcomes grid and make notes of any ideas that have come to you about them through the exercise.

Swap roles and start the exercise again

The exercise takes different amounts of time for different pairs of participants. I allow students to take a break at the conclusion of both scenarios which means they can leave quietly in pairs so that others can continue with their scenes. Students came back into the larger group at the end to discuss, evaluate and debrief the exercise. The two sessions I have so far run took two hours with around half an hour dedicated to each landscape. In the second session I took photographs of some of the landscapes. I have reflected that in future sessions I will ask students to take photographs of their landscapes with a digital camera I provide.

Analysis of learning outcomes

Since becoming an Academic Tutor my attention has focussed on the well documented dilemma of how to help students see the relevance of theory and recognise it within their practice:

> A monumental challenge for many students concerns the use of theories, methods, frameworks and models in the practice setting. So often students – and indeed practitioners – will avoid theories, state they do not see their relevance, or even actively renounce them. However, theories and models guide social workers' actions and provide explanatory frameworks that make effective interventions possible and, in doing so, they contribute to ethical, evidence-based and accountable practice. (Parker, 2006, p.17)

In developing the sand tray exercise for a practice seminar group I wanted to attempt to give students the opportunity to reflect on module learning outcomes to help them begin to examine the frameworks and methodologies governing practice. Each student had a worksheet in their handouts containing a grid of placement module learning outcomes. I asked students to explore links to their reflections about the sand tray exercise with knowledge and theory identified through the practice module learning outcomes. In the feedback session with their partner I asked students to share any links to theory they identified. One student focussed on a critical incident in her placement where a long standing member of staff was consistently being overtly racist and discriminatory towards adults with severe and enduring mental health problems. Her subsequent disclosure about various incidents to her Practice Teacher caused a great deal of anxiety for her as a new practitioner in her first placement. As she and her partner explored the sand tray landscape they were able to identify ethical dilemmas and the unique position of social worker values that helped her to feel less anxious about taking action. I discussed the incident individually with the student and she very kindly wrote the following for inclusion in this article:

The sand tray exercise was very timely. It was the week before I was to meet with my practice teacher and the supervisor to discuss the situation and I was, quite frankly, terrified.

The exercise, and the following discussion, helped me to see the links between the theories of anti-discriminatory practice and how this works in practice and what it means. In other words, it showed me the implications and even consequences of working in an anti-discriminatory way – it is not enough to pay homage to rhetoric, but it means taking risks and sometimes taking very difficult action. It brought home to me the reality. The exercise also helped me to understand the theory behind the identity of a social worker – to me that means values, knowledge and skills that are unique to social workers. Again, I began to understand how important this identity is and that it is necessary to stand apart when service user's experiences are at stake. Theory made real. Finally, it helped me to understand that performance management, which in the past had seemed a bit ridiculous, when done properly is a very important part of practice. Reflection is the most important part of social work, and the sand tray exercise, which appeared to be a bit of fun and an experiment, proved to be an exceptional tool for good reflection to take place.

This student had been concerned about the outcome of taking action when she perceived her position as powerless when measured against that of an experienced member of staff from whom she was supposed to be learning. In fact the student describes a feeling of being 'terrified'. In her article beginning with the words, 'It's not that I'm no good it's just that I'm scared …'. Howath (1999) discusses the importance of managing anxiety effectively in practice learning to facilitate 'functional learning cycles'. The student's confidence seemed boosted by the sand tray exercise and she recognised the importance of challenging racism and anti discriminatory practice through channels designed to protect workers and people who use services. The student had a supportive Practice Teacher who stood beside her through an active process of investigating the incidents, another important link in developing robust professionalism.

Other students built case studies in the sand and discussed how powerful it was in their feedback to the group. As I watched the sand tray landscapes emerge in the sessions they appeared to portray signs of powerlessness and hopelessness. I observed islands, walls of sand, figures hidden behind hills or cut off. Conversely, what followed in the feedback of narratives were mostly feelings of hope and understanding; ideas about solutions and future action. Here is realised the importance of non-interpretive intervention, the inherent rule of projective play therapy. In the moment of intuitive creation, lies the revelations, the potential solutions, the ways forward, the human condition of optimism and surety of finding a way through. Over the two sessions I ran with two different sets of students I heard them discussing parenting and child protection, family systems, working within the health sector, organisational structures, social justice and some of the conflicts between the humanistic values in social work and the modernisation agenda. Students fed back that they saw the potential of using the sand tray as a Direct Work tool. Further, many students demonstrated that they were already beginning to develop a sense of the importance of examining personal values and the part they play in promoting social justice and ethical professional practice. This was good learning for me as I reflected on the motivation that exists for people who wish to become social workers and their intentions to promote the best interests of people they work with.

Evaluations and feedback

Immediate feedback from both sessions demonstrated that students felt they had undertaken a powerful exercise that had deepened their knowledge of their work. Two students described how they removed the sand tray from their desks and went and sat on the floor, giving them a real sense of play. Other students agreed they enjoyed the playful aspects of the exercise and using creativity to think about their cases. Some students said they had come with an open mind, or a certain amount of scepticism. The following are some comments from the evaluation sheets which were completed by all 10 students at the second session:

It made me look. Good to see how I placed myself within the situation.

It helped me see my case outside of my head i.e. distance myself temporarily and be objective........good exercise – exceeded my expectations.

I saw how useful this tool is. Feel it would be appropriate to use it with service users.

Great exercise. Open to individual interpretation.

I went into the session very open minded and was impressed with how powerful the session was.

Very interested, very sceptical before the session however, this changed as I found it very useful to visualise the case scenario in depth.

A good vehicle for discussing difficult cases.

Something in uni that's fun at last!

About half the group said that the exercise had helped them reflect on learning outcomes, others said they were more interested in seeing the landscape and how it might help them in their practice. Comments on the evaluation sheets about links with module learning outcomes varied:

Not many outcomes linked to my scene but useful to reflect on them.

Helpful to link the session to learning outcomes.

....struggled relating it to context and practices learning outcomes

I really enjoyed this session; it was useful, helped greatly with the learning outcomes and gave me some good ideas.

I got out of this what I needed and asked for i.e. linked practice to learning outcomes.

This article has been very upbeat and positive about the learning opportunities offered by the sand tray exercise. However, I am more than aware that some of my group tend to avoid small group sessions and I have a sense of an 'opt out' element. Howath's (1999) discussion of dysfunctional and functional learning cycles is of relevance here in establishing what motivates students and what might be 'scaring them off'. I might also add that seminars appear to have a 'bolt on' rather than 'integral' feel with issues including being timetabled on a Friday and being held at very irregular intervals throughout the course. Seminars may appear to students to add a further burden to an already full timetable.

I have duly noted that many of students who did come to the session expressed some scepticism about the usefulness of the exercise, perhaps they were also understandably anxious about a tool which may ask them to confront the more emotional and difficult aspects of the social work task. In the first session a student asked if the exercise was a psychological test and I needed to reassure him. He was very nervous about taking on the role of facilitator with the other student. The student gave very positive feedback on learning at the end of the session. My hope is that 'word of mouth' and this article may provide encouragement. I will need to do more research on student motivation.

Reflecting on the exercise has become an important aspect of my own practice in delivering this session, as well as deepening my knowledge about what students may need in their learning to practice reflectivity. I have for example recognised the significance of being a motivator, innovator and leader in adult education to help students get the very best out of learning. In the sand tray exercise, being a 'teacher' requires a process of letting go of traditional 'teaching roles' and finding ways to hand learning over to students. My reflections on both sessions were that the crucial elements of my work were in setting the scene for an exercise that belonged to the group. I saw my role as holding the space, answering any questions and ensuring the space was respected, which it was without my help. My action for the next session is to ensure I ask students how they see my role while the exercise is being carried out. Do they want me to remain in the room, do they want me to wander about and observe, would they prefer me to sit in a corner only helping them when they ask for it?

Conclusion

The success of the sand tray exercise lies in its value as an intuitive and expressive tool that can be used therapeutically across a range of settings to promote an understanding of our place in 'all this'. The sand tray is a tool for focussing on what is going on and provides a space to potentially resolve, or solve difficulties or make links for ourselves. Sand Play is a projective play process developed by Lowenfeld outside of the traditional psychodynamic techniques traditionally used in psychoanalysis. Thus projective play allows the process to belong to the maker and honours their narrative of it. Projective play techniques have transferred to use with adults through the growth of Jungian and Gestalt Therapy. The sand tray exercise is experienced first hand by the student/practitioner so they too can come to understand the intrinsic value of 'self' within a process. Having experienced the tool as a Direct Worker with children and as a Practice Teacher I saw its potential as a small group teaching tool. I developed a sand tray session that I hoped would allow students to examine an intuitively made landscape about their practice and link it to a knowledge and value base as well as learning outcomes. Immediate feedback and evaluation with students indicates that there was some success at linking theory, practice and learning outcomes. The exercise has also shown itself to be a rich source of learning for student/practitioners, many of whom were sceptical about its value. The feedback has inspired me to go on developing the sand tray tool to help students reflect on practice.

The development of reflective practice in Higher Education has demonstrated the benefits that can be derived from deep learning processes. In social work the complexity of relationships between practitioner, student, professions and organisations with service users requires a thorough approach in examining practice values that empower as well as uphold human dignity and social justice. Yet opening up practice to scrutiny comes with potential anxieties for students and practitioners about the very frameworks designed to uphold transparent practice to deliver services. Reflective practices have to be developed that allow practitioner/students to safely explore values, belief systems and self knowledge. Students also need to examine learning processes connected to knowledge. In beginning to develop the sand tray seminar it is my hope that this is a tool will contribute to innovative practice in reflective processes in social work education.

References

Brockbank, A. and MacGill, I. (2000) *Facilitating Reflective Learning in Higher Education* Buckingham: Open University Press

De Domenico, G. (1995) *Sand Tray-World Play/a comprehensive guide to the use of the sand tray in psychotherapeutic and transformational settings.* Oakland, Ca: Vision Quest Images (accessed at http://vision-quest.us/VQISR/Sandtray-Worldplay_The%20Tool_.pdf)

De Domenico, G. (2002) Sandtray-WorldplayTM: A Psychotherapeutic and transformational Sandplay Technique for Individuals, Couples, Families and Groups *The Sandtray Network Journal* [accessed at www.sandtray.org/publications page, or direct access at http://vision-quest.us/vqisr/The%20Sandtray-Worldplay%20Method%20of%20Sandplay.pdf]

General Social Care Council (2006). *Assuring Quality for Child Care Social Work.* London: GSCC

Gibbs, G. (1985) *Teaching Students to Learn.* Buckingham: Open University Press

Gibbs, G. (1988) *Learning by Doing. A guide to teaching and learning methods.* Oxford: Oxford Polytechnic

Gould, N. and Baldwin, M (Eds.) 2004. *Social Work, Critical Reflection and the Learning Organisation.* Aldershot:Ashgate

Howath, J. (1999) It's not that I'm no good it's just that I'm scared: Managing anxiety associated with practice learning. *Issues in Social Work Education,* 19, 1, 17-35

Kolb, D.A. (1984) *Experiential Learning.* Englewood Cliffs, NJ. Prentice Hall

Lowenfeld, M. (1967) *Play in childhood.* New York: Wiley (accessed at http://www.sandtray.com/history.htm)

Oaklander, V. (1978) *Windows to Our Children.* Highland, NY: The Gestalt Journal Press

Parker, J. (2006) *Effective Practice Learning in Social Work.* Exeter: Learning Matters

Schon, D.A. (1987). *Educating the Reflective Practitioner* San Francisco: Jossey-Bass

Stevens, C. (2004) Playing in the sand *The British Gestalt Journal,* 13, 1, 18-23

Taylor, C. (2006) Narrating the significant experience: Reflective accounts and the production of (self) knowledge. *British Journal of Social Work,* 36, 189-206

Yip, K. 2006 Self reflection in reflective practice: a note of caution.. *British Journal of Social Work,* 36, 777-788

Web Site References

All website addresses were accessed and available on 15th Oct 2007
http://www.calplaytherapy.org/trainings.html
http://vision-quest.us/vqisr/The%20Sandtray-Worldplay%20Method%20of%20Sandplay.pdf. Based on *Sand tray Network Journal*, (2002), 6, 1
http://www.mappmed.co.uk/Workshops/SandPlayTherapy/PlayingintheSandPublishedPaper/tabid/59/Default.aspx (Christine Stevens article – see References above)

Social work practice with Arab Muslim women living in Western societies

Bassima Schbley[1] and Mark Kaufman[2]

Summary: This article discusses how practice teachers and others involved in social work education can enhance the quality of services being provided to Arab Muslim women living in Western societies. It draws upon the relevant literature, as well as the results of a small-scale survey by the lead author of Arab Muslim women living in the United States. The authors argue that social work learning cannot be separated from the influence of culture, which sometimes includes religious beliefs and practices.

Keywords: cultural competence; Arab Muslim women; social work practice

1. Assistant Professor, Dept of Social Work, Washburn University, Topeka, Kansas
2. Associate Professor, Dept of Social Work, Washburn University, Topeka, Kansas

Address for Correspondence: Bassima Schbley, Dept of Social Work, Washburn University, 1700 College Avenue, Topeka, KS 66621, USA. bassima.schbley@washburn.edu

Introduction

During the past 15 years, there has been an increasing recognition within social work and the other social service professions in Europe and North America that 'more emphasis should be placed on training students for cultural competence during their field work' (Kaufman and Love, 2003, p.30). This period has seen an increase in the academic literature devoted to this topic in Great Britain (e.g. Humphries, 1998), France (e.g. Ion and Ravon, 2001), the United States (e.g. Lum, 2000), and many other countries as well (e.g. Healy, 2001). The value of this literature has been recognized, both in general terms (Corey, Corey and Callanan, 2003) and in its specific contribution to advances in areas such as anti-oppressive practice (Issitt, 1999). However, this growing literature has also been criticized for not sufficiently providing practice teachers and classroom teachers with 'down-to-earth practical ideas which are readily adaptable to students' needs and abilities' (Ronnau, 1994, pp.30–31). For example, one practice learning coordinator in Great Britain questioned 'whether practice teachers and others in social work education are giving sufficient attention to assisting students to explore the potential significance of religion to ... the lives and perspectives of service users' (Gilligan, 2003, p.75).

This lack of attention to the significance of religion in the lives of some service users is a matter of concern, given the complex and contrasting trends toward both secularism and religiosity in the countries of Western Europe and North America. Furness (2003) observed that 'Britain has witnessed over the past forty years declining numbers of people who attend [Christian] church ... in contrast to Pakistani and Bangladeshi Muslims who still place religion central to their lives' (p.62). Consequently, 'social work in Britain takes place in a diverse society made up of people ranging from those for whom religious beliefs and traditions determine and dominate their whole way of life ... to those who would say that it had little or no influence on their actions and behaviors' (p.62). Gilligan (2003) similarly noted that 'in Britain ... for a large and increasing number of service users, religion is a basic aspect of human experience, both within and outside the context of religious institutions' (p.77). Despite this fact, Gilligan's recent survey research 'tends to reinforce the earlier impression that social work has not, and is not, giving issues of religion and belief priority in the education and training of social workers' (p.80). He argues that 'practice teachers need to urgently review their practice with regard to the exploration of issues concerning religion and belief with students, if they are to become competent social workers' (p.75).

Our article is a response to this increasing recognition that more emphasis should be placed on training students for cultural competence in their field work, including competence in understanding the impact of religious beliefs and practices on the lives of clients. We focus on the social service needs of Arab Muslim women who were born and raised in the Middle East, but who are now living in Western societies. We focus on this client population for four reasons. First, developing the knowledge and confidence to effectively provide services to any culturally diverse group is a skill set that should generalize, to some degree, to all minority clients. Second, developing these skills vis-à-vis Arab Muslim women should particularly generalize to more effective service delivery to other Muslim clients (non-Arabs, and men), a growing segment of minority clients in Western societies. Third, the service needs of Arab Muslim women often are particularly challenging, given the frequently difficult transition from growing up in a very 'traditional' religious culture and then relocating to a largely secular Western society. Fourth, the lead author of this article was raised as an Arab Muslim woman in Lebanon until age 16, has lived for many years in the United States, and has a long-standing interest in the topics explored in this article. This interest was spurred further by a review of two recent research studies (both supported, at least in part, by the United Nations) that examined the increasingly challenging problems faced by Arab Muslim women in an era of religious fundamentalism in their countries of origin. The current article will discuss the results of the lead author's recent survey research with 15 Arab Muslim women who relocated to the United States from Lebanon. The details of this research both confirm and elaborate upon the United Nations–sponsored studies, which will also be examined.

This article consists of three sections. First, we briefly summarize some of the recent academic literature on multicultural social work practice, emphasizing the elements of that literature that are most relevant to this article. Second, we present the lead author's recent original research findings, the results of the 15 in-depth interviews referred to above. Third, we discuss some of the specific implications of this research for practice teaching and social work education.

Multicultural social work literature and religion

Noting the relatively small amount of published material on either religious beliefs or spirituality that is specifically aimed at social workers, Gilligan (2003) observed that 'to talk about religion and spirituality is for many people as embarrassing as talking about sex, death and money' (p.78). Despite this, he argues that, for clients seeking social services, these are issues that sometimes need to be talked about, and with sensitivity and competence. In fact, as Crompton (1998) reminded us, the Children Act of 1989 in Great Britain highlighted the law's expectation that social workers will give explicit attention to the religious needs of young clients, when appropriate.

Of course, it is not always easy to determine when such attention is appropriate. On the one hand, Patel, Naik, and Humphries (1998) emphasized that 'religious cultural practices' and 'religion as therapy' have 'no place in social work education and practice' (p.ii). Instead, these authors advocated for a more informed understanding of religious differences and for social work students to become better prepared to practice in a pluralistic society. On the other hand, while fully recognizing that social work must protect its boundaries and remain a wholly secular profession, Derezotes (1995) observed that the religious and spiritual values of clients will sometimes influence the assessment and intervention strategies developed by social workers. Attempting to find the right balance, Gilligan (2003) observed; 'There is clearly an ... unresolved confusion amongst many social workers and social work educators about what role discussion of religion and belief can play, in an apparently "modern" and "secular" age, and more especially in the context of a commitment to anti-oppressive practice' (p.76).

Some efforts to address this confusion have been productive. For example, Furness (2003) conducted a small-scale survey with social work students in Bradford, England, to elicit their views about the impact of faith and belief on social work practice. Focusing on the significant Muslim population in Bradford, Furness warned against the 'misconception that all Muslims and Asians are a homogeneous group and that they share very similar traditions and customs' (p.63). The author described a picture of 'commonalities, differences, and [the] separate nature of these diverse communities' (p.63). These are themes to which we will return in the next section of our article.

Other studies have sought to introduce some clarity to this challenging topic by developing cohesive frameworks to guide multicultural social work practice. For example, Kaufman and Love (2003), in an extensive review of the British and North American social work literature on multicultural practice, concluded that three themes frequently recur. First, many studies stress the importance of the practitioner's awareness of his or her own cultural values and biases. Second, it is vital to recognize that a culturally competent practitioner seeks to understand the worldview and culture of the client, and possesses at least some specific knowledge of diverse client groups and of relevant sociopolitical influences. Third, the effective practitioner should possess specific skills and intervention techniques to serve culturally diverse clients. We will return to these three themes later in this article.

Next, however, we examine recent research that should help practitioners better understand the service needs of Arab Muslim women now living in Western societies. We are not the first to examine the service needs of a particular group. For example, the British social work literature has examined the specific psychosocial needs of racial minorities (Kirton, 1999), and the academic literature has helped social workers in Spain to work more effectively with immigrants to that country (Pacheco, Plaza, Fernandez-Ramirez and Andres, 2003). There is an extensive social work literature in the United States focusing on the specific needs of Spanish-speaking immigrants (Beckett and Dungee-Anderson, 1996).

Research results:
Arab Muslim women in Western societies

An impetus for our own survey research on this topic, conducted in 2003, has been the *Human Development Report* issued intermittently (in 1985, 1988, 1992, 1994, 1996, and 2000) by the United Nations Development Program (2000). Over the past two decades these authoritative reports have utilized 62 socioeconomic, medical, and political 'indicators' to conduct cross-cultural analyses of the world's developing countries. These reports present a stark picture of the declining status and well-being of Arab Muslim women in Lebanon. These women are being forced back into the confinement of their families and away from opportunities in the public sphere of community and national affairs that Lebanon's past had provided (see also Shehadeh, 1998). The reason for these changes certainly appears to have been the dramatic resurgence of religious fundamentalism over the past 20 years among large segments of the Lebanese Muslim population (Joseph, 1994). The effects of this resurgence are reflected in the U.N. *Human Development Report* of 2000. According to this report, less than 45% of Muslim Lebanese women were employed outside the home; that figure had been 60% in 1980. In 2000, the average salary of Muslim Lebanese men was 85% higher than that of Muslim Lebanese women; this percentage had been 47% in 1980.

To suggest that some versions of religious fundamentalism may pose challenges to some of the typical social development goals encouraged by the social work profession is not meant to suggest that these religious affiliations fail to meet other human needs. We certainly do not wish to imply that anyone should be prohibited from any type of religious affiliation. Nor are we suggesting that Islamic religious fundamentalism is unique among religions in raising concerns related to social development goals. Social work values require that all such issues be addressed with tolerance and respect. We stress that the issues discussed in this article are simply examples of the challenges that confront social workers in pluralistic Western societies when working with clients who were raised in very traditional religious societies.

The lead author solicited participation in a qualitatively oriented interview process from Muslim Lebanese-born adult women who had lived in Lebanon at least until 1995, and who were currently residing in Wichita, Kansas (a Midwestern U.S. city with a population of approximately 370,000). Participation was sought from 15 such women from various socioeconomic backgrounds for in-depth interviews focusing on many aspects of their life experience both in Lebanon and in the United States. One-page flyers that explained the purpose of the study and that solicited volunteers were posted at the local Wichita Muslim Community Center. To reduce any 'cohort effect' (related to age and socioeconomic status), basic demographic information was collected from each of the initial respondents to the flyers. Fifteen volunteers were then selected from among all of the respondents, with an effort to reduce any cohort effect. Nonetheless, the participants obviously did 'self-select' by volunteering initially, and the interviewees cannot be viewed as a fully random sample of all Muslim Lebanese women living in Wichita, Kansas (or in the United States, of course).

The 15 participants ranged in age from 19 to 69, and all were currently married (except for the 69-year-old participant, who was divorced). There was a significant degree of socioeconomic diversity. Three of the women were very poor and were receiving poverty-related public welfare benefits. Two women were employed and viewed their job as supplementing their husband's income. Three women owned their own businesses. Five women were married to engineering or medical professionals and two women were financially supported by their adult children. The effort to recruit women from various Islamic religious sects was also successful: nine women were affiliated with the Sunni Abbassy sect, three with the Shia Jafary sect, two with the Suni Hanafy sect, and one with the Shia Twelvers sect. This pattern was expected because these are the most common Islamic sects both in Lebanon and in Wichita, Kansas.

The qualitative design for these open-ended interviews was guided by a dual emphasis on 'narrative-interpretive theory' (Marshall and Rossman, 1999) and the 'feminist critical theory paradigm' (Fine, 1992; Rubin and Babbie, 2001; Stewart, 2001). Feminist critical theory focuses on the interplay of power between genders and also seeks to be sensitive to the potential interplay of power between researcher and research participant. This focus seemed of particular importance to the lead author because she was once an 'insider' (born in Lebanon and lived there until age 16) who is now more of an 'outsider.' All interviews were conducted in Arabic, the primary language of all the participants. However, many of the participants' thoughts and expressions were uttered in English. All interviews were audiotaped. Fully informed consent was obtained from each participant, which permits utilization of all data, although without any reference to the names of participants or significantly identifying descriptions. The audiotaping was used only for documentation, translation, and interpretation of the data. The lead author subsequently listened to each audiotape and translated each one from oral Lebanese Arabic into written English. After each interview, the lead author recorded her personal reflections in a journal in an effort to monitor her own reactions to the interview, to identify possible biases, and to reflect on how she might alleviate any such biased questioning during subsequent interviews.

Each transcript was reviewed several times in order to identify common themes, which were then labeled as such (Morrow and Smith, 2000).

Seventeen common themes were identified and grouped in three broad categories: (1) the role of the interviewees as Lebanese Muslim women, wives, and citizens; (2) a discussion of their education, employment, and overall life satisfaction; and (3) the impact of religion on their lives. Because our findings are quite similar to those of an impressive and influential wide-scale research project that recounts similar narratives of Arab Muslim women from Egypt, Jordan, Tunisia, Yemen, and the Palestinian Territories (Jabre, Underwood and Goodsmith, 1997), we discuss the findings from our study and the other study together (noting the study to which we are referring). Jabre et al's (1997) research was an advocacy and training project intended to promote and document women's empowerment and active participation in social development in the Arab world. It was 'carried out with support from the United States Agency for International Development, the European Commission, and the Arab Gulf Programme for United Nations Development Organizations' (Jabre, Underwood and Goodsmith, 1997, p.iii).

Each of the 15 women in our study and each of the 30 women profiled in the study by Jabre et al appear to view their achievements and their struggles within the broader context of their families and communities. This was the most remarkably consistent theme within and between the studies. Jabre et al observed:

> In Arab culture, the individual is more deeply embedded in a closely connected social network than in most Western contexts, and becomes actualized by being part of, and working for, the well-being of the group. Rather than being measured by Western standards of personal success and individual gratification, achievement is recognized chiefly through contributions made within this familial and social context. (p.93)

Similarly, Jacobson (1994) observed that:

> Western notions of autonomy based on the concepts of privacy and individual rights ... may be less relevant to Muslim women, who value the interdependence of individuals, families, and communities. (p.26)

We discuss additional findings of our own survey research in the following section of our article, which focuses on various implications for practice teaching and social work education.

Implications for practice teaching and social work education

Several findings from our study have significant implications for practice teaching and social work education. One of the most significant findings was that few of the participants in our study seemed willing to jeopardize their marriages or compromise their roles as mothers and daughters by harshly criticizing their social and religious milieu, despite referring to various inequities. For example, some participants noted that Islam mandates that a Muslim woman must submit to the will of her husband or father, as long as these men do not contradict Islamic law ('Sharia'). Participants in our study reported numerous incidents in Lebanon in which female friends and family members were either divorced or fired from jobs for defying religious prohibitions, or for nonconformance with dress codes. Others were punished merely for using perfume. Many had been prohibited from higher education, restricted from driving automobiles, and forced into marriage. Our participants and those in the study by Jabre, Underwood and Goodsmith frequently described their need to focus on resolving the tensions between their personal needs and their perceived family responsibilities.

The result of these tensions, as Jabre and colleagues (1997) insightfully observed, is a 'complex blending of respect for, and resistance to, established traditions' (p.93). Most of the women in our study referred both to a stronger religious affiliation and to greater life satisfaction since moving to the United States. Clearly they also appreciated the increased economic opportunities. They tended to explain their higher levels of overt religiosity while living in Wichita, Kansas, as in part a reaction to perceived hostility toward Islam by many in the United States, particularly since September 11, 2001. Some felt the need to affirm their Islamic heritage by wearing a veil. At the same time, however, many of these women expressed an ongoing concern about the resurgence of religious fundamentalism in Lebanon.

Another significant finding of our study with major implications for practice teaching and social work education is that most of the participants in our study had already stepped outside traditional roles and found new opportunities, including employment, community volunteer work, and social and political activism. Most of the participants in our study had vigorously pursued these new opportunities in the United

States, and some had begun this effort while still living in Lebanon. This was again also true for the majority of the participants in the study by Jabre, et al.

What factors had encouraged these women to pursue such opportunities? Many of the women mentioned receiving emotional support from family members, particularly husbands and fathers. Given traditional expectations about female roles, there were some inevitable tensions when these women became involved in matters outside the home. To avoid these problems, some women chose to marry men who supported their personal goals and outside involvements. When tensions did arise, most of the women in both studies turned to the arts of persuasion and negotiation. Rather than directly challenging their husband's position as head of the family, they sought to maintain family harmony. They pursued a 'gradualist' strategy to eventually obtain the support of their husbands. Social workers who develop a familiarity with and sensitivity toward the typical relationship patterns of Arab Muslim families may sometimes be in a position to facilitate such productive negotiations.

In their efforts to pursue personal goals, many of the women in these two studies also received emotional and practical support from friends and neighbours. Such informal social networks are not constrained by rigid hierarchies and can be quite facilitating. Again, the sensitive and well-trained social worker may be in a position to make a positive contribution to this process. As Jabre, Underwood and Goodsmith (1997) observed:

> Bringing women who have led relatively isolated lives into a group with a clearly defined purpose – such as a literacy class or a small business loan program – begins a process that neither the individual nor the group's sponsor may have foreseen.... [T]he accomplishments of each woman in a group serve as an inspirational and practical model for others to emulate. (p.104)

We conclude this section with specific suggestions about how our research findings can be usefully applied by practice teachers and other social work educators. In linking our findings to the practice teaching and learning process, we refer again to the various dimensions of effective multicultural social work practice discussed by Kaufman and Love (2003). They argue that there is value in teaching students about specific strategies, skills, and interventions that seem appropriate for specific minority clients, and helping students to become more aware of the impact of their own cultural values, and more aware of the worldview and culture of their clients.

Practice teachers and educators should strive to create an atmosphere in which cultural differences can be explored and questions asked. We have described the very different family culture and political atmosphere in which many Arab Muslim women clients have been raised. It is not reasonable to expect most social work students to be fully conversant about such issues. However, the practice teacher should help the student to identify the kind of information that is required to understand what is going on in the helping situation. Following Pinderhughes (1989), we encourage practice teachers to seek exploration of the following issues when their students are working with Arab Muslim women who were raised in the Middle East:

1. To what extent is the presenting problem related to issues of transition, such as immigration?
2. Is the behavior at issue considered normal within the client's own culture, or is it considered dysfunctional?
3. To what extent is the current problem a manifestation of lack of access to resources and environmental supports?
4. To what extent is the problem related to culture conflict in identity, values, or relationships?
5. Is the client a participant in any Muslim organizations that have been particularly helpful?
6. What are the other available cultural strengths and resources, such as cultural practices, social networks, and family support systems?

Regarding the sixth point, practice teachers should encourage their students to actively seek out opportunities in the community to learn about Arab and Muslim culture, because our research findings (and other research as well) point to some significant differences from Western cultures. In many communities, a wide variety of cultural events occur throughout the year, and many of them will be available at minimal or no cost to students. If the practice teacher periodically informs students about these events, it 'serves as a reminder that cultural awareness is valued, is an ongoing process, and requires active involvement' (Ronnau, 1994, p.35). Students also should be encouraged to listen to music and read books and poetry by Muslim Arabs. Students might usefully visit other agencies that specifically serve Arab Muslim clients, such as refugee programs, women's centers, advocacy groups, and community centers.

Finally, our research findings demonstrate the importance that Arab Muslim women place on their connection to extended helping networks within their own communities. Therefore, practice teachers and classroom teachers should consider inviting respected members of that community to meet with students in order to explain how cultural and religious factors might influence how clients perceive the social agency's programs and services. Such diversity training workshops can make use of the skills of community leaders who will be found in many cities. In a similar vein, our research suggests that practice teachers should encourage their students to make the fullest possible use of appropriate indigenous sources of helping within the client's own community. Social services usually are enhanced when practitioners have learned how to incorporate naturally occurring support systems. This includes the extended family system, as well as the broader religious community. At times, it may be appropriate to seek consultation with religious leaders in the community.

Conclusion

Jabre, Underwood and Goodsmith (1997) concluded their study with a set of recommendations for social service professionals who seek to enhance the personal and social development goals of Arab Muslim women. These recommendations include the following: (1) offer access to new ideas, information, and resources; (2) foster social support for women's education and their active participation in public life; and (3) help women better understand their legal rights and how to obtain them (pp.117–118). These appear to be thoughtful, appropriate recommendations, assuming that they are pursued with tact and sensitivity, and with a recognition of the family dynamics that may create challenges for such a pursuit.

Ahmad (1996) reminds us that 'cultural norms provide guidelines for understanding and action, guidelines which are flexible and changing, open to different interpretations across people and across time, structured by gender, class, and other contexts' (p.190). We also concur with Gilligan's (2003) reminder that 'for practice teachers and for social work students ... learning cannot be separated from the influence of context and culture, including religion and belief' (p.85). We encourage practice teachers and other educators to proceed with a commitment to social justice, and with the confidence that their efforts will contribute to increased social cohesion in our rapidly integrating world community.

References

Ahmad, W. (1996) The trouble with culture, in D. Kelleher and S. Hillier (Eds.) *Researching Cultural Differences in Health* . London: Routledge (pp.190-219)

Beckett, J.O. and Dungee-Anderson, D. (1996) A framework for agency-based multicultural training and supervision. *Journal of Multicultural Social Work,* 4, 4, 27-48

Corey, G., Corey, M.S., and Callanan, P. (2003) *Issues and Ethics in the Helping Professions.* Pacific Grove, CA: Wadsworth

Crompton, M. (1998) *Children, Spirituality, Religion and Social Work.* Aldershot: Ashgate

Derezotes, D.S. (1995) Spirituality and religiosity: Neglected factors in social work practice. *Arete,* 20, 1, 1-15

Fine, M. (1992) *Disruptive Voices: the Possibilities of Feminist Research.* Ann Arbor, MI: University of Michigan Press

Furness, S. (2003) Religion, beliefs and culturally competent social work practice. *Journal of Practice Teaching,* 5, 1, 61-74

Gilligan, P. (2003) 'It isn't discussed.' Religion, belief and practice teaching: Missing components of cultural competence in social work education. *Journal of Practice Teaching,* 5, 1, 75-95

Healy, L.M. (2001) *International Social Work: Professional action in an interdependent world.* New York: Oxford University Press

Humphries, B. (1998) Contemporary practice learning in social work: Tensions and possibilities. *Journal of Practice Teaching,* 1, 2, 4-12

Ion, J. and Ravon, B. (2001) *Les Travailleurs sociaux.* Paris: La Decouverte

Issitt, M. (1999) Towards the development of anti-oppressive practice: the challenge for multi-disciplinary working. *Journal of Practice Teaching,* 2, 2, 21-36

Jabre, B., Underwood, C., and Goodsmith, L. (1997) *Arab Women Speak Out: Profiles in self-empowerment.* Baltimore, MD: Johns Hopkins University School of Public Health

Jacobson, J. (1994) *Family, Gender, and Population Policy: Views from the Middle East.* New York: The Population Council

Joseph, S. (1994) Problematizing gender and relational rights: Experiences from Lebanon. *Social Politics,* 1, 3, 271-285

Kaufman, M. and Love, D. (2003) Recent trends in multicultural practice: Implications for practice teaching and field education. *Journal of Practice Teaching,* 4, 3, 29-53

Kirton, D. (1999) Perspectives on race and adoption: The views of student social workers. *British Journal of Social Work,* 29, 779-796

Lum, D. (2000) *Social Work Practice and People of Color.* Belmont, California: Brooks/Cole

Marshall, C. and Rossman, G. (1999) *Designing Qualitative Research.* Thousand Oaks, California: Sage Publications

Morrow, S. and Smith, M. (2000) Qualitative research for counseling psychology, in S.D. Brown and R.W. Lent (Eds.) *Handbook of Counseling Psychology.* New York: Wiley (pp.199-230)

Pacheco, E.R., Plaza, S.H., Fernandez-Ramirez, B., and Andres, P.C. (2003) The implications of immigration for the training of social work professionals in Spain. *British Journal of Social Work,* 33, 49-65

Patel, N., Naik, D., and Humphries, B. (Eds.). (1998) *Visions of Reality, Religion and Ethnicity in Social Work.* London: CCETSW

Pinderhughes, E. (1989). *Understanding Race, Ethnicity, and Power.* New York: The Free Press

Ronnau, J.P. (1994) Teaching cultural competence: Practical ideas for social work educators. *Journal of Multicultural Social Work,* 3, 1, 29-42

Rubin, A. and Babbie, E. (2001) *Research Methods for Social Work.* Belmont, CA: Brooks-Cole

Shehadeh, L. (1998) The legal status of married women in Lebanon. *International Journal for Middle Eastern Studies,* 30, 501-519

Stewart, A. (2001) *Theorizing Feminism: Parallel trends in the humanities and social sciences.* Boulder, CO: Westview Press

United Nations Development Program. (2000) *Human Development Report.* Retrieved May 24, 2002, from http://www.undp.org.1b/

Failing to fail students in the caring professions: Is the assessment process failing the professions?

Mike Shapton[1]

Summary: This article represents a personal view of the phenomenon of professionals 'failing to fail' students of questionable competence. It is mainly drawn from the author's experience first as a practice teacher, then as a lecturer and manager of a social work qualifying programme and recently as tutor of a programme preparing social workers and others to become practice teachers and assessors. The article first examines aspects of the process of practice assessment and then argues that the turnover amongst those given this responsibility means that the expertise appropriate to undertaking such a complex task is difficult to accumulate. It then offers some remedies that focus more on organisational responses than simply on the individual professionals who take on this essential responsibility.

Much of the recent concern about social work practice teaching and assessing has focussed on the question of quantity. Getting enough practice learning opportunities is a perennial problem in itself- but this article addresses an issue of quality, namely ensuring that both pass and fail decisions are made with confidence.

As the author's background is social work in England, the article will use social work terminology and refer to social work and other documents from the English context, but he hopes that readers from other professions and countries will find the debate useful.

This article is developed from a talk given by the author at the fifth International Conference on Practice Teaching and Field Education in Health and Social Work, York, 10-12 July 2006.

Keywords: assessment; failing; practice learning

1. Course Director, Practice Education Programme, Coventry University

Address for Correspondence: Dept of Social & Community Studies, Richard Crossman Building, Coventry University, Coventry CV1 5FB. m.shapton@coventry.ac.uk

Introduction

In the UK, social work follows a model of professional learning where academic study is combined with periods of practice learning and the award of a professionally accredited higher education qualification effectively facilitates admission to the profession. (A contrasting example is the legal profession where universities offer academic degrees and the profession controls the processes leading to professional competence.) There is an increasingly overt emphasis on the value of practice learning as the key to raising the status of the social work profession. An example of this comes from Stephen Ladyman, Parliamentary Under Secretary of State for Community talking about the new social work degree introduced in 2003:

> The quantity and quality of practice learning opportunities available to students will be critical in achieving a better trained workforce.' (Ladyman, 2004)

One of the initiatives to achieve this critical outcome was the establishment of the Practice Learning Taskforce, whose Annual Report 2004/5 predicted 'an increase in demand for practice learning of between 39-118%' (cited in Doel, 2006, p.7). Inevitably this is leading to the involvement of many new people in practice learning to meet this increase in quantity. This article, however, addresses an issue of quality important to the overall objective of enhancing social work's professional status.

It is not difficult to hear anecdotal evidence from human service professionals of students not deemed competent in practice still gaining professional qualifications. A detailed study undertaken on behalf of the Nursing and Midwifery Council (Duffy, 2003) produced a useful analysis of this phenomenon, much of which, I believe, could be replicated by a study of social work practice learning. Duffy cites Watson and Harris (1999) reporting that 46% of nurse mentors agreed with the suggestion that some students passed placements despite unsatisfactory performance.

One of the issues that may strike the reader of Duffy's report is the number and complexity of the factors which lead to situations of failing to fail. She did achieve a broad categorisation of reasons as follows (2003, p.47)

- *Leaving it too late* covers a number of process issues
- *Personal consequences* mainly refers to negative impact on the student
- *Facing personal challenges* refers to the negative impact on the mentor
- *Experience and confidence* relates to the uncertainty about standards more common among inexperienced mentors.

A similar picture is reported by Furness and Gilligan (2004) in respect of assessments of social work students. Yet these failures to fail are being admitted to by experienced, competent professionals who spend their working lives making decisions affecting the health and welfare of many thousands of people. In comparison, it is rare to find academics declaring, for example, 'that failing a student was a difficult thing to do and that personal, emotional as well as practical issues influenced the outcome of their judgements' (Duffy, 2003, p.5).

I would suggest that an additional dimension in the failing to fail phenomenon, certainly for social work, is the question of resources. In their article drawing on 'our own direct experience and on discussions between over 70 practice teachers, tutors and placement co-ordinators' Furness and Gilligan (2004. p. 465) point to the current context of inadequate resources and insufficient recognition for the task of teaching and assessing social work students. The resource argument is often debated but progress is rare and inadequate. Employers find themselves in a vicious circle of a shortfall of social workers to do the social work task (see, for example, Parker & Whitfield, 2006), making it constantly difficult to release them to teach and assess the practice of the growing number of students recruited to courses to address that same shortfall.

As each social work student must have experience in at least two practice settings, the need for an increased quantity of practice learning opportunities has led to the involvement of many other professionals who also need opportunities to understand the social work role for which students are preparing. It is notable that the minimum criteria to assess a social work student do not stipulate any training (GSCC, 2002a), and, although it is usual to offer training, it varies from two days upwards. It is also significant that the GSCC (2002a, p.19) requires

that those responsible for the *final* [my emphasis] assessment that a student is qualified to practice include experienced social workers and professional educators.

On the basis of these requirements, students can progress a considerable way through their 200 days of practice learning without being assessed by a qualified and experienced social worker.

The present article is modest in its aspirations and does not make unrealistic claims for a large switch of resources to practice teaching. Some of what is said is based on my perceptions rather than researched evidence, for as Duffy (2003. p.5) says, 'the area of failing students ... has received very little attention'. However it is hoped that the article may prompt worthwhile local debates on the practice assessment processes prevailing on social work and similar courses and may result in research in social work education of a similar nature to Duffy's.

For the conference talk which preceded the article I was invited to blame either practice or the universities for the 'failure to fail'. I considered this suggestion unproductive, but it triggered a comparison of aspects of practice and academic assessment which might prove helpful as many practice assessors will not have direct experience of academic assessment and vice versa. As I believe a fuller mutual appreciation of the issues might generate some solutions, the comparison is reproduced here. The intention is to promote co-operation, not to compete for who faces the greater challenge, and to focus the perceptions of practitioners and academics alike on the nature of the task of practice assessment compared to academic assessment in an organisational context. A shared perception may enable both groups to work more pro-actively to enhance both the quantity and effectiveness of resources devoted to practice assessment and minimise obstacles to reaching the right assessment decision. The analysis inevitably generalises about both practice and academic processes, and while I recognise there will be differing practices in some contexts, I believe the generalities merit consideration.

The assessment process

Seven aspects of the assessment process are considered:

- The focus of assessment
- The methods of assessment
- Moderation of assessment
- Re-assessment following failure
- Assessment regulations
- Relationships with the assessed
- The personnel involved

The focus of assessment

Academic focus	Practice focus
'The measure of knowledge, understanding and skills.' (QAA, 2006, para.12)	'The measure of knowledge, skills and *behaviour*.' (Carpenter, 2004)
Single subject modules as building blocks.	Many or all standards in each practice learning opportunity.

The first point of comparison is the focus of assessment. The first key difference is that in practice there is a need to assess behaviour, rarely a focus of academic assessment. Note that Carpenter differentiates between skills and behaviour. I would interpret behaviour as both the ethical dimension of a student's practice and the aggregation of skills into methods of working: how they are doing the job. The second key difference is that this behaviour is expressed in terms of 21 units clustered in six key roles. (TOPSS, 2002) plus a Code of Practice (GSCC, 2002b) to which social work students should adhere once registered as students with the GSCC (General Social Care Council). Assessment in a social work placement is against a significant number, if not all 21, of these. Given that approved behaviour among human service professionals is inherently varied, deciding when a student's behaviour is so unacceptable or short of competence to be classed as failing rather than a learning need involves a complex judgement. In comparison a lecturer is usually focussing on a limited number of learning outcomes from a defined component of the academic curriculum (i.e a module) as demonstrated in one or more delineated assessment tasks (QAA, 2006, para.13).

The methods of assessment

Academic focus	Practice focus
Standardised learning opportunities	Learning opportunities individualised and interpreted
Tasks often indicative rather than exhaustive.	Tasks potentially very wide (wider than reflected in portfolios)
Standardised assessment tasks.	Standardised requirements open to interpretation.
Student authored material	Combination of material from student and others

To develop the last point further, the next comparison focuses on the impact of the individuality and complexity of the methods of assessment in the practice setting. The key roles and Code of Practice are inevitably written in such a way that both the learning opportunities and the assessment which follows need interpreting in each separate specific practice context. The range of activities undertaken by the student is potentially very wide (much more so than requires evidencing in the typical practice assessment portfolio) and the material which is required for the typical portfolio is a combination of material created by the student and material from others – the practice assessor, her colleagues, people from other professions and service users. In comparison, an academic module usually offers standardised learning opportunities (lectures, seminars, guided study etc), standardised assessment tasks which are indicative of learning achieved and almost all material assessed is student authored.

Moderation of assessment: Checking the evidence

Academic focus	Practice focus
Assessment material about knowledge, understanding (and some skills) is often fixed and open to review	Assessment material about skills and behaviour is mainly based on transitory events. Only the records of these events are open to review.

Considerable emphasis is placed on the quality assurance of academic assessment achieved by both internal and external moderation. Internal and external moderators can see the original or a copy of a student's written material along with the first marker's comments to ensure adherence to standards. Much of the most valuable evidence of behaviour and performance in practice is transitory, and once observed, can only be recorded in the account of one or more of the parties involved. Permanent, first-hand evidence such as video- and audio-recording remains unpopular with assessors, and even if popularised, could only record what many assessors regard as 'set piece' practice. Much valuable evidence of both competent and incompetent practice is seen and absorbed, but may only be patchily recalled if needed, and challenged for this reason by a student fighting to establish their competence. Therefore it is not easy for moderation processes to verify original evidence and be sure of the standards used by practice assessors to interpret what they see.

Re-assessment following failure

Academic focus	Practice focus
Re-assessment usually involves the resubmission of the original assessment tasks or something similar, or re-attendance at the next delivery of the module, either option having negligible resource implications	Re-assessment of practice (beyond remedying portfolio deficits, which is rarely grounds for failure) usually involves extending a placement or locating an extra one with significant resource implications

In the event of student failure in an academic module, the resource implications for the course and the university are usually minimal – perhaps a little extra tutorial time, but the resource implications for practice failure are potentially considerable in the context of the chronic scarcity of placements repeatedly cited around the country. In fact it is not unknown for university regulations to be much more restrictive about 're-sit' opportunities for practice as opposed to academic modules (for example at one university local to the author, final year academic modules can be reassessed or studied again as of right, but for the final placement this right does not exist and further assessment opportunities can only be agreed by the Programme Assessment Board under exceptional circumstances).

Assessment regulations: 'The rules of engagement'

Academic focus	Practice focus
Academic regulations are complex, but familiarity comes with time to HEI staff.	Learning a particular HEI's regulations in detail is not a priority task.
Interpretations of regulations are transmitted through the informal network.	Interpretation of HEI regulations is more difficult to communicate

Many practice assessors accept students from more than one university or other Higher Education Institution (HEI), or the period between accepting students is such that if they had committed to memory some of the regulations, they may have forgotten them next time around. Most university courses will supply a handbook either with the regulations or a guide to them, but in the midst of the other concerns of a practice assessor, especially one with a struggling student, they may be slow to turn to the procedures. In addition, most practice assessors, unless they have sustained involvement with the university will not have been party to any prior discussion of the interpretation of those regulations. In contrast, over time, academics acquire increased understanding of the university regulations they use most, and their interpretation, and can anticipate responses to students in difficulties (just as practitioners become familiar with law and procedure). Duffy (2003, p.28) reported that 'not following procedure is a major factor as to why some students are passing practice placements without having demonstrated sufficient competence'.

Relationships with the assessed

Academic focus	Practice focus
Academic assessors are likely to have little or no personal relationship with the student. Assessable work may be anonymised	Practice assessors have a close personal relationship with the student, have personally managed the student's learning and accountability

Personal relationships between students and academic lecturers are of variable intensity depending on a number of factors such as how many modules lecturer and student are jointly engaged in, whether the lecturer is personal tutor to a particular student, and how much a particular student engages with a particular lecturer. It is possible that a lecturer marking a student's work cannot even recall a face to put to a name, or anonymisation of work masks the identity of even a lecturer's personal tutees. In contrast a practice assessor usually takes the major responsibility for organising the learning opportunities which precede student practice assessment, is likely to have come to know a great deal about the student as a person and provided emotional as well as practical support through the challenges of learning to practise social work. Confronting a student with a fail recommendation after such an experience can be a daunting prospect.

The personnel involved

Academic focus	Practice focus
Comparatively constant staff group	Constantly changing personnel
Teach students in groups	Most take one student at a time
Usually in same or connected locations	Scattered locations limited networking.
Primary role is education	Primary role is Practice

It is commonly recognised that the turnover in practice assessors is considerable. People move to other jobs where taking students is not feasible, or simply do not continue offering placements for a number of reasons (see, for example, Furness and Gilligan, 2004, p.467; Kearney, 2003, p.4). The most common model of practice assessing is to have one student at a time, and perhaps not have another for a year at least. Practice assessors are scattered across a range of organisations in social work and social care. The primary role of most practice assessors is social work or care work and not practice education. These factors militate against the accumulation of expertise and confidence in the roles of teaching and assessment, and it is in the difficult area of marginal and failing students that expertise and confidence is most needed. In contrast, lecturers are in the business of education – of teaching and assessing, of passing and failing. Newcomers receive induction and support and are assimilated into the academic culture. Social work teaching teams are often comparatively small and often located in the same building, accelerating the assimilation of the newcomer. Expertise and confidence in the key educational tasks grows at the rate one expects of anyone in their primary occupational role.

Two possible remedies

Arising from the above analysis, I would like to offer two possible remedies, the first focussing on practice learning providers and the second on HEIs' strategy for practice assessment. The GSCC states that '(t)he degree in social work prepares students for employment as professionally qualified social workers' and consequently the universities are required both to award the degree and to 'secure, approve, allocate and audit appropriate practice learning opportunities'(GSCC, 2002a). For this reason, HEIs should concern themselves with both remedies.

Promoting and developing a strong community of practice.

The last aspect of the analysis (the personnel involved) highlighted the fragmentation of the practice assessing community. Wenger's (1998) concept of 'communities of practice' offers a useful vehicle for analysing the situation and offering one pragmatic remedy. He presents a social theory of learning that focuses on learning as social participation, and suggests we all belong to several socially participating groups, which is what he calls communities of practice. (Practice here effectively means 'activity' rather than, say, social work practice or educational practice.) Practice, he argues, defines a community through three dimensions: mutual engagement, a joint enterprise and a shared repertoire (Wenger, 1998, p.152). These dimensions are summarised in the figure below. It is in our communities of practice that a new professional, for example, a social worker or nurse extends, reinforces and refines the learning gained when qualifying. 'When we are with a community of practice of which we are a full member we are in familiar territory' (p.152). Wenger suggests that 'the boundaries of our communities manifest as a lack of competence' (p.153).

Dimensions of a community of practice, after Wenger (1998)

Mutual engagement
In a community of practice we learn:
- How to engage, as practice teachers/assessors with other people.
- How to interact with others and work together.
- What part we can play within this community.
- What identity we gain through being part of this community.

Joint enterprise
- Shared perspectives generate certain interpretations, actions and responses.
- This sense of joint enterprise can lead us to value certain experiences, and make certain choices.
- A shared identity tends to generate shared perspectives.

Shared repertoire
- Sustained engagement in an activity facilitates the ability to interpret and use a wider repertoire.
- The repertoire is built from the history of actions, the language and the concepts we absorb and contribute to.
- The repertoire becomes more personalised through experience

If we need social workers to feel competent in their assessments of students and overcome the problems identified by Duffy (2003) and summarised earlier, we need to enable them to be sufficiently and consistently engaged in learning and assessment issues to form part of a community of practice. This will consolidate their learning and also enable them to contribute to their colleagues' development in this area of activity. Wenger presents the 'community of practice' as a naturally occurring social phenomenon, but I would suggest that its benefits are such that we might consider strategies to help foster their development.

Few organisations have developed retention strategies for practice teachers (Lindsay & Walton, 2000), and often staff take what expertise they have gained into parallel roles of staff supervision and management or some move into academia (for example, Kearney, 2003; Lindsay & Tompsett, 1998). While this may benefit social work generally, it hinders the development of high levels of expertise in practice learning. Doel (2006) reports characteristics of English local authorities demonstrating success in practice learning and it is easy to see how some of these characteristics would foster 'communities of practice': They have champions of practice learning; they embed the function in job roles; they provide meaningful incentives and a programme of training and support; they have strong partnerships with HEI's (who of course have a parallel academic community of practice). Parker and Whitfield (2006) encourage others to follow this successful strategy.

Some organisations that provide large numbers of good quality student placements, such as those surveyed by Doel (op cit.) create combined posts, perhaps half practitioner, half practice teacher and in others, full-time practice teacher posts exist. Such postholders can provide a centre to Wenger's 'community', but we need to keep other staff involved frequently enough to give to and take from the 'community'. This means organisations, developing strategies to keep practitioners who start taking students involved over a longer period of time. It helps further if the larger organisations can help smaller ones in the locality by including them in their development or foster a similar community-building strategy. The HEIs too can negotiate a contributory role (a factor already identified in successful local authorities).

A critical review by universities of their management of practice assessment

The second remedy to consider relates to the experience of practitioners who recommend that a student fails a practice module. Many practitioners perceive that a recommendation to fail a student will trigger a reaction much more demanding of them than the reaction to a lecturer failing an assignment for an academic module. They anticipate extra demands on their time (which may already have been stretched by protecting the service users' and agency's interests in the context of a student struggling with competence), and scrutiny of the quality of the learning opportunities they provided. Duffy (2003) reported experiences of this nature. In contrast, a modest number of fails in an academic module assignment is seen as routine and rarely triggers any scrutiny beyond standard moderation processes. In addition, practice assessors are often unsure of the university's response, which often comes initially via the student's personal tutor. The personal tutor in fact may see themselves as having a variety of agendas, including maximising the university pass rate and advocating on behalf of the student. While tutors would wish to see themselves as allied with practice assessors in safeguarding professional standards, they may not be perceived as helping practice assessors with the technically and emotionally demanding task of seeing through a fail recommendation. Undoubtedly there will be variation between universities in how far they have developed practice assessment strategies which take account of the way practice assessment processes differ from academic assessment, but I would invite all universities to ask themselves some questions about their strategy on practice assessment:

- Do we attach the same level of importance to the assessment of practice as to academic assessment?
- Do we ensure that we apply the same level of quality assurance to practice assessment as we do to academic assessment?
- Do we ensure that practice assessors have full and timely information about factors affecting a student's likely performance, e.g. needs arising from a disability or concerns raised by a previous practice assessor?
- Do we have regulations and procedures that make it more difficult for re-assessment in practice compared to academic re-assessment?

- Do we communicate our regulations and procedures on failing students as effectively as possible so that practitioners can rapidly understand what is entailed?
- Do we ensure that a practice assessor working with a struggling student has access to experienced consultancy acquainted with the particular university's processes from someone who is not also expected to advocate for the student?
- Do we have a strategy for advocating that a practice assessor working with a struggling student is given extra time to meet the demands of concluding that experience in as positive a way as possible for all concerned?
- Do we recognise the impact on a practice assessor of questioning the quality of a placement after already approving its use by placing a student there?

Conclusion

At the beginning of this article I argued that the issue, failing to fail, was important to the quality of enhancing professional status. It is also important at a much more local and personal level: how incompetent professionals impact on their organisations, on their close working colleagues, and most importantly on the public, the users of their services. Duffy's very illuminating research rightly attracted some interest from the professional and general press (see NMC, 2004; BBC, 2004; Guardian Unlimited, 2004). Sadly the emphasis the press chose was to say to nurses 'must try harder'. The press personalised a difficulty which, I argue, should be analysed systemically. The professions need to validate the importance of the task they entrust to those who teach and assess the next generation of practitioners and build expertise. The universities need to be proactive in supporting that strategy so that they have confidence in the practice assessment recommendations they receive. They need too, to ensure that the process for handling student failure in practice recognises the challenges of the task and that there is a reliable strategy to support practice assessors to achieve the right outcome for the profession. I hope that the issues addressed will stimulate debate and act as a trigger for further research on the topic.

References

BBC (2004) *Warning over sub-standard nurses.* May 12, 2004. bbc.co.uk

Carpenter, J (2004) *How Can We Evaluate the Outcomes of Social Work Education?* Presentation given at the Joint Social Work Education Conference, Glasgow, July 2004

Doel, M. (2006) *Effective Practice Teaching in Local Authorities, (1).* Practice Leaning Taskforce Capturing the Learning series. London: Skills for Care

Duffy, K (2003) *Failing Students: A qualitative study of factors that influence the decisions regarding assessment of students' competence in practice* http://www.nmc-uk.org/aFrameDisplay.aspx?DocumentID=1330

Furness, S. and Gilligan, P. (2004) Fit for purpose: Issues from practice placements, practice teaching and the assessment of students' practice. *Social Work Education,* 23, 4, 465-479

GSCC (General Social Care Council) (2002a) *Accreditation of Universities to Grant Degrees in Social Work.* London: GSCC

GSCC (General Social Care Council) (2002b) *Codes of Practice for Social Care Workers and Employers.* London: GSCC

Guardian Unlimited (2004) Nurses 'allow incompetent students to qualify'. www.society.guardian.co.uk, May 12th

Kearney, P. (2003) *A framework for Supporting and Assessing Practice Learning.* London: Social Care Institute for Excellence

Ladyman, S, (2004) Speech given as Parliamentary Under Secretary of State for Community, 16 July 2004*: Improvement and Development Agency - Learning Exchange on the Theme of Supporting Social Care Workers* www.dh.gov.uk/NewsHome/Speeches/SpeechesList/SpeechesArticle/fs/en?CONTENT_ID=4088005andchk=FrhIRY

Lindsay, J and Tompsett, H. (1998) *Careers of Practice Teachers in the London and South East region.* London: CCETSW

Lindsay, J. and Walton, A (2000) *Workforce Planning and the Strategic Development of Practice Teachers in Approved Agencies in the CCETSW England Regulation 1999.* London: CCETSW/Kingston University

NMC (Nursing and Midwifery Council) (2004) *Nurse mentors need to learn to fail nurses* NMC press release 6 May 2004, www.epolitix.com/NR/rdonlyres/74FD5E36-4D41-4EES-9AYA-7B2E266D074E/0/NMC

Parker, J. and Whitfield, J. (2006) *Effective Practice Teaching in Local Authorities, (2),* Practice Leaning Taskforce Capturing the Learning series. London: Skills for CareQAA (Quality Assurance Agency) (2006) *Code of practice for the assurance of academic quality and standards in higher education: Assessment of students, second edition,* (www,qaa.ac.uk/public/cop/COPassessment)

TOPSS (Training Organisation for the Personal Social Services) (2002) *National Occupational Standards for Social Work* (www.topss.org.uk/uk_eng/standards/cdrom/Index.htm) [This document is now more easily accessed on the website of the successor organisation to TOPSS: www.skillsforcare.org.uk]

Watson, H.E. and Harris, B. (1999) *Supporting Students in Practice Placements in Scotland* Glasgow Caledonian University: Dept of Nursing and Community Health cited in Duffy, K. (2003)

Wenger, E. (1998) *Communities of Practice.* Cambridge: Cambridge University Press

Human geography and questions for social work education

Pat Wilkinson[1] & Gavin Bissell[2]

Summary: Despite a sometimes implied lead, in the social work literature, of social work training over health training in the area of values, since the decline of community social work in the 1980s health training has developed a focus upon the physical environment which seems set to leave social work education trailing behind in the area. This paper therefore explores inter - professional overlap in the area of human geography, and in particular its relation to professional identity and the core social work value of social responsibility. Finally, it outlines ways of raising awareness of the physical environment among social work students, and in doing so seeks to break free of the placement/learning environment dichotomy and link social responsibility to the campus experience itself.

Keywords: human geography; space; placement learning; social work education; environment

1. Head of Department and Senior University Teacher
2. University Teacher

Address for Correspondence: Gavin Bissell, Dept of Social Sciences and Humanities, University of Bradford, Bradford BD7 1DP, UK. g.bissell@bradford.ac.uk

Introduction

A popular phrase in the social sciences in the 1990s was 'space makes a difference', as the regionally varied impact of economic and structural change in Britain during that period was investigated. Although there was no agreement upon exactly what difference it did make, the impact that the localities debate had upon sociology, cultural studies, and health studies in the 1980s and 1990s was notable (Giddens, 1984; Urry, 1985; Peet & Thrift, 1989; Duncan, 1989; Paasi, 1991; Jackson, 1991; Sayer, 1991; Duncan & Savage, 1991), and spatial concepts now seem to occupy a modest but permanent place in these areas (Phillipson, 2007; Popay et al, 2003; Gillespie, 2002; Andrews, 2006). There are even signs of a renewal of interest in recent years (Duncan, 2002).

Yet the impact of this 'geographical turn' upon social work has been more muted, and this is especially true of human geography, which concerns itself primarily with perceptions of place. The purpose of this paper is therefore to explore one small aspect of the relationship between social work and place, and that is its role in practice learning. In fact the regulating body of social work requires that the placement be a 'conducive physical environment', and of course this means more than merely being a 'safe' place: is it for example experienced as a place conducive to learning? Does the student feel at home, or uneasy, at the placement agency? More to the point perhaps, do service users? This is the area we are looking at.

Fortunately we can draw upon parallel initiatives in doing this. Lessons can be learned from Health Studies (see Curtis & Rees-Jones, 1998 for a useful summary), from the HEFCE Sustainability in Education agenda, and from existing techniques in geography education.

The campus and social work values

We want to start by looking at what the universities' sustainability agenda can contribute to this area, and then move on to the contribution of Health Studies.

It is now accepted that the geography of the university campus will play an important role in inculcating the values of environmental responsibility in the next generation of graduates (Martin & Wheeler,

1975; Bahro, 1986; Cahill, 2002). What is much less certain, however, is how the equally important values of social responsibility are to be passed on to the next generation. That goal was, in fact, one legacy of the early - twentieth - century University Settlement Movement, the proponents of which, Jane Addams, Patrick Geddes and others, are often seen as involved in the early history of social work in Britain and America (Addams, 1910/1967; Geddes, 1915/1968). Their envisioned method of inculcating social responsibility, the *summum bonum* of student houses sited in the community, has faded. Where to now?

The question is more pressing than it might at first appear. A third of students now remain living at home for the duration of their degrees, and because of this many will miss altogether the important and often formative experience of being a new arrival in an unfamiliar area. Even those who do in growing numbers swell the student cohorts of distant city universities, however, will probably begin and perhaps spend their study years elsewhere than in the formative melange of a student house squeezed between terraced family homes. Instead, they will as likely as not find themselves cocooned in secure and comparatively luxurious study bedrooms, removed from the streets and environment that Jane Addams and Patrick Geddes saw as so essential to the development of social responsibility (Addams, 1910/1967; Geddes, 1915/1968).

In this paper, other ramifications of the situation will be explored, and some possible ways forward identified.

Consequences of the student ghetto

This should not be read as a nostalgic piece about better times, since a system of privileged access for a minority but funded by all could hardly command general respect in the present political climate. Yet there are senses in which the present arrangement does not necessarily appear more democratic. For example, the heterogenizing intentions of the University Settlement Movement were partly realized insofar as some class permeability occurred in Settlement areas, and partly realized later in the areas in which students lodged amongst diverse groups (Addams, 1910/1967; Geddes, 1915/1968). With the increasing creation of whole areas exclusively populated by young students, however, it is possible to find students turning away from other groups and associating exclusively with one another. At the same time, the absence of other groups such as buggy-pushers and long-term residents leaves students little concerned about street refuse, poor pavements and building sites. Diverse groups such as new arrivals, older people, and those with disabilities, will have (been) removed to other sites.

Geddes (1915/1968) also felt strongly that travel should be a learning event, perhaps at its best in the daily walk or bus ride, and here again experiences will be diverse.

It might be objected that we have no clear idea of what a campus environment that inculcates social responsibility would look like. We do have some fairly well established clues, however. Sommer (1974) observed the individualizing construction of new university campuses in America in the 1960s, with their fixed forward-facing lecture room seating, their concentration on individual study facilities, their alienating architecture, and their often remote campus location which tends to encourage dispersion and departure after 4pm for staff and many students. These findings, taken together with Addams' (1910/1967) Settlement Movement ideals, suggest the following. The 'socially responsible' campus should be outward-looking, non-individualizing, co-operative and anti-oppressive, and should involve students, staff *and others* in the life of the university. It can, and most universities do, achieve this to a varying extent by existing strategies. For example, theatres, galleries, some libraries, gymnasia, swimming pools, refectories and even bars on campus have guest access or better, and taken together with concerts, school visits, sports events, conferences and fixed ceremonies, they ensure that universities are outward-looking to at least some extent, although there is arguably a class basis to community participation in educational institution informal activities (Bagnall et al., 2003).

However, the 'socially responsible' campus must link students up to whatever community involvement it has, as well as engaging students in the life of the university, and this is not straightforward, as Sommer (1974) found.

From the point of view of social work training, we could draw in the travel-to-campus experience, draw in the ongoing job-based experience of undergraduates, and make more of course representatives and other forms of student involvement.

Summarizing, student involvement issues are geographical issues, as well as social ones, partly because the human geography of the campus is not always conducive to collective projects and to engagement.

Placements as a site for the inculcation of social responsibility

It might well be objected that the social work placement now furnishes the physical environment in which the student encounters the service user more or less against the physical backdrop of the service user's own territory. There are at least two significant problems with this view.

Firstly, the view sets up an implicit opposition between a neutral learning environment in the university, on one hand, and the physical environment of social work beyond the campus wall, on the other. However, Sommer's (1974) 'new campus' research in the 1970s led him to infer that the perception of a neutral learning environment on university campuses resulted from the desensitization of individuals to their environment, rather than neutrality *per se*. The notion of 'unconscious' use of space in a campus context was further developed by Lym (1980) with the distinction between 'acute' and 'chronic' experiences of space, with 'chronic' experience of space implying an unreflecting or even indifferent movement between locations.

Secondly, the 'placement encounter' view of place awareness presupposes that the physical environment of social work is in fact detected in a meaningful way: that it involves an 'acute' experience of space, to put it in Lym's (1980) terms. Yet we will have to divert our attention to Health Service training to get some idea of what we are looking for here.

Health and the environment

The Black Report (1981) linked health outcomes to social class, and in the Nineteen - Eighties this was taken on board in community work and to an extent in social work. In the late 1980s a revival of interest in health and the environment took place, but this renewed interest in the environment seems not to have had quite the same impact in social work as it has in Health Studies. Why not? One reason may be that social work seemed to have substituted the rather abstract notion of the 'community', in the form of The NHS and Community Care Act (1990), for the real physical environment of local streets and buildings. The result is that the physical environment increasingly appears as a virtual entity in social work. Moreover, social work seems to have by-passed the debate in the social sciences in the 1980s, in which the fruitful but arguably static and otherwise problematic geographical concepts embodied in Community Studies in the 1970s were transformed, in the 1980s, first into Locality Studies and then into complex conceptions of culture, place, and Habitus (Massey & Jess, 1995).

At the same time, and in marked contrast, health trusts have implemented community development programs over the same period which have highlighted the relevance of the physical environment (Plant & McFeely, 2004). Perhaps symptomatically, the Journal *Health & Place*, which began in 1995, appears to have no social work equivalent, and the teaching model used in nurse education seems to take the physical environment of nursing students themselves into consideration, even to the extent of supervising their general living conditions (Abbatt & McMahon, 1985). When it comes to the outcome of training, Healy et al. (2003) have identified what appear to be significant differences in the environmental awareness of Nurses, Social Workers, and Occupational Therapists, with the latter seeming to show the greatest awareness of the physical environment when making hospital discharge arrangements. The NHS, furthermore, appears to be funding research into its own organizational environment (Halford & Leonard, 2005). However we interpret their findings, they do seem to suggest that the health care approach possesses important advantages in this area.

Social work and the environment

Social work does have a geographical tradition, but it seems much more tentative, provisional and scattered (Gutheil, 1992; Resnick & Jaffee, 1982; Germain, 1978; Phillipson, 2007). This is particularly interesting if somewhat ironical in view of the perceived inclusiveness and flexibility of the social work knowledge base.

Indeed, social workers are perceived by health colleagues, according to health - originated research findings, as having a fuzzy knowledge base and therefore some uncertainty regarding their professional identity and their role in multi-disciplinary teams, which in turn is seen to lead to lower levels of professional confidence and uncertainty in dealing with patients (Carpenter et al, 2003).

Conversely, social workers tend to see their health colleagues as sometimes placing too much confidence in a putative 'medical model' and consequently 'knowing what is best' for individual service users (Bircher, 2000; Oliver & Sapey, 1999). They point to the provisional and apparently changing nature of the health advice given out by community medicine practitioners as evidence of the misplaced confidence of health colleagues, and more recently they question the power of the Pharmaceutical industry and its role in the determination of medical practice with service users (Green, 1982; Phillipson, 1989; Law, 2006). Finally, Social workers have an incipient fear that their job is being taken over by the medical model (Carey, 2003; Butler & Drakeford, 2005).

Despite the picture of professional divergence which this suggests, however, we want to argue that there are potential gains for social work in the encounter between social work and health care, and that a key positive is the attention given to the person-environment relation. The question then is: how can social workers overcome the professional reluctance to focus upon the environment, tied as it is to our perception of ourselves as primarily workers with human relationships? More precisely, how can such a change be developed in the classroom?

Pedagogic methods for raising awareness of the social work placement environment

This section of the paper is about level of awareness, and students' ability to relate perceptions of the campus to social work issues and to the placement.

An earlier study with 20 MA Social Work students found relatively low levels of awareness of placement geography issues (Wilkinson & Bissell, 2005). The problem seemed to be that those students who already had an awareness of placement geography answered questions about it comprehensively, but these students were a tiny minority. The problem therefore seemed to be that students' awareness of placement geography depended upon the individual student being sensitive to geographical features prior to the start of the placement. If they didn't have this, we found, there was little to be gained by engaging them in exercises and discussions about the physical features of the placement either during or following completion of the placement. We therefore conjectured that it was necessary to raise student awareness of aspects of the physical environment-principally issues of risk, oppression, and identity-*before* they went out on placement. It should then be possible to engage students in discussion of these aspects of their placement during and after the placement experience. The problem at this stage was that of how to raise awareness of appropriate aspects of the physical environment. Any training exercise had to involve all 66 students in discussion.

There are several techniques in the literature on environmental education, with approaches such as (preparing and participating in) town trails and guided urban walks (Martin & Wheeler, 1975). It is interesting to note in this connection that Birmingham University social work students as long ago as the 1960's were boarded onto coaches and escorted around deprived areas of the city as part of their induction.

The campus experience seemed an obvious place experience common to all of us (though there were others), and this formed the subject of the first exercise. Fortunately there was a social work literature to draw upon at this point (Adams, Geddes), and we were also able to connect with recent work upon the relation between the pedagogic physical environment and the inculcation of ethics (Bahro, 1986), some of it emerging from the Ecoversity project at Bradford University.

The Ecoversity project

The Ecoversity project at Bradford University is based upon the notion that if sustainable and environment-conscious features are part of the campus environment then this will help to produce graduates who are similarly aware. There is currently a competition to see who can come up with the best design for a new 500-bed green student village on the campus, and one issue will be whether students will actually prefer private luxury single study flats to collective environmentally-conscious student houses.

From the point of view of training social workers, if we can use a physical environment to inculcate environmental responsibility, then we can also use it to promote social responsibility, on the reasonable expectation that once stimulated the sense of responsibility can be extended. But social responsibility is inextricably linked with environmental responsibility anyway: it may be of limited effect to ask a disadvantaged person to prioritize ecologically sound waste disposal and consumption while accommodation, unemployment, family needs or debt are immediate concerns.

We acknowledge, too, that if social workers are to be trained in environmental perception then they may also need to be assessed in it, which may add to the agenda of training offered to practice educators and others. But does this necessarily move us away from the National Occupational Standards-led breakdown of the social work role? Arguably not: indeed the values, for example, only fully make sense insofar as they are applied to social work with people in specific physical environments. As Duncan (1991) has pointed out, social relations do not exist 'on the head of a pin'. A more extensive analysis of the relation of human geography to the NOPS key roles and values, however, is beyond the scope of the present article.

The Campus exercise

The pre-placement students were given an A3-sized map of the University campus, and invited to identify on the map places about which they had various kinds of feelings. This exercise is based upon a spatial awareness-raising map exercise used by Stea (1976) with schoolchildren. Stea (1976) noted incidentally that adults typically have lower levels of spatial awareness than children.

We then hoped to carry out a similar exercise around the same students' placement experiences, once these were underway. This part of the study is still in progress: overall, we hope it will raise student awareness of placement human geography, and with it awareness of the impact of the physical environment of welfare agencies upon service users.

There were some interesting initial findings with the map exercise, however, which are worth summarizing briefly here, since they shed a little light on the place awareness of a cohort of first year social work students.

When asked to identify places on the campus they tended to avoid, students identified: the nearby college entrance; the student common room, which they perceived to be used by students from non-social work degree pathways and/or students from the college; areas of the campus, such as behind the sports hall, frequented by students from other faculties (for example computer studies students, rightly or wrongly perceived to have a 'laddish' culture oriented to 'male' interests such as football or cars), or by college students; or by non-students.

These three experiences were widespread, and seemed to be more about social class than anything else, although gender may have been an involved factor. They seemed not to be about ethnicity.

Some students identified one particular corner of the campus as a place they avoided late at night. When questioned further, they said that this was where students from two separate halls of residence clashed when going to and from the students' union on the campus. Geographically, it was the point at which the pathways merged. One hall was off-campus. The apparent place-identities of these two groups of students are very interesting, and worth further study.

When asked to identify a place where they went for privacy and quiet study, many students identified a coffee bar on the campus, and also the refectory, and the usually sunny Atrium. It is interesting that they did not identify the library, in view of the fact that library architecture is specifically designed to promote privacy (Sommer, 1974). This finding is however consistent with Lym's (1980) findings, which highlighted the social usage of university libraries.

Conversely, when asked to identify a place where they felt most relaxed and safe, most students identified the library. Arguably, this fits in well with research done on identity and place: the library is perhaps the place where students get most confirmation of their identity, and therefore feel most secure and relaxed (Relph, 1976).

Interestingly, students identified a variety of places they went to at lunchtime, including a bar area and outside bar area on the campus, even though they did not go there to drink alcohol. The outside bar area was of interest to smokers, but also to others. Also, some students clearly ate their lunch in the library, even though it was against regulations, and went there with their friends, suggesting that it was an important social location too.

So far, the responses and explanations given by students in class support the view that users' perceptions of a place do not necessarily coincide with its ostensible purpose, and this is an important, if obvious, message for students to take with them to their placement agencies

(Taylor, 1974).

Generally, students tended to identify areas well - in on the campus as safe relaxed places where they felt at home or had their lunch, and opted to see the edges of the campus or just outside it as places that they tend to avoid. There were exceptions: one student identified no less than seven places as lunch locations (including a car park and a grass bank), apparently having a well-developed sense of place where food was concerned.

This avoidance of the immediate environs of the campus among first-year undergraduates may be nothing more than the inward-looking nature of the university as a psychological entity (Sommer, 1974). However, in the case of social work students, it perhaps feeds into the implicit opposition between welfare placement on one hand and neutral learning environment on the other, described earlier as an implicit feature of social work training courses.

Some methodological questions present themselves at this point. It is assumed that all students can read the map: they have after all been using it to locate classrooms for most of the year, presumably. It might be objected that spatial experience is three-dimensional, whilst the mapping exercise is two dimensional. It has been pointed out by Campbell (1994) that primary experience of place is in fact two-dimensional, and that individual orientation to place is not within 'absolute' space, but in relation to the 'slope' of a place or its primary directionality for the individual. The questions about purpose ('Where would you go for privacy..') key in to this directionality or slope. These questions around the application of concepts lead to the larger question of the under-use of human geography in social work and whether or not this arises from the use of interpretive methods. There is current debate in the human geography literature itself about the apparently marginal status of this discipline and the reasons for it (Cameron, 2005). On one hand, it is seen to preoccupy itself with abstract and 'irrelevant' issues, whilst on the other, it is perceived to be naïve in its apparently uncritical acceptance of such politically loaded concepts as 'underclass' Cameron, 2005). Do these problems arise from the interpretive nature of human geography, however, and is Human Geography to be avoided by social work researchers because it is interpretive in nature? This does not appear to have been an obstacle to the 'interpretive turn' in, for example, the critical criminology of the 1970's, and Ward (1973) seemed to acknowledge a potential role for human geography in that area at that time. Or is it that geography itself continues to be tacitly thought insufficiently critical for social work research purposes (Hurst, 1985)?

Conclusion

The overall argument of this paper can be summed up as follows. The social work literature identifies a diverse corpus of theories – in tension – as its knowledge base, and sees this as an asset, distancing itself from what it takes to be the orthodoxy of medical scientism. Despite this diversity in the knowledge base, however, the opportunity to engage with the study of the physical environment of social work, and of social work education, has not been fully grasped. The campus environment of social work education may provide an opportunity to develop social work students' missing awareness of the physical environment, an awareness which can then be carried forward to social work placements, with potential benefits for service users. In this regard, the specific initiative of the Ecoversity may offer a unique conjunction at which to engage students' attention with the campus physical milieu, reconnecting social work education with its earlier traditions of the Settlement Movement and community engagement.

References

Abbatt, F. and McMahon, R. (1985) *Teaching Health Care Workers. A practical guide.* London. Macmillan

Addams, J. (1967) *Twenty Years at Hull House.* New York: Macmillan. (Original edition, 1910)

Andrews, G. (2006) Geographies of health in nursing. *Health & Place,* 12, 1, 110-118

Bagnall, G., Longhurst, B., and Savage,M. (2003) Children, belonging and social capital: the PTA and middle class narratives of social involvement in the North West of England. *Sociological Research Online,* 8, 4

Bahro, R. (1986). *Building The Green Movement.* London: GMP

Bircher, G. (2000) Disabled people, health professionals. *Disability & Society,* 15, 5, 775-783

Cahill, M. 2002. *Environment and Welfare: Towards a green social policy.* Basingstoke: Palgrave Macmillan

Cameron, A. (2005) Geographies of welfare and exclusion: Initial report. *Progress in Human Geography* 29, 2, 194-203

Campbell, J. (1994) *Past, Space, and Self.* London. MIT Press

Carey, M. (2002) Anatomy of a care manager. *Work, Employment and Society*, 17, 1, 121-135

Carpenter, J., Schneider, J., Brandon, T., and Wooff, D. (2003) Working in multidisciplinary community mental health teams: The impact on social workers and health professionals of integrated mental health care. *British Journal of Social Work,* 33, 8, 1081-1103

Curtis, S. & Rees-Jones, (1998) Is there a place for geography in the analysis of health inequality? in M. Bartley, D. Blane, and G.D. Smith (Eds.) *The Sociology Of Health Inequalities.* Oxford: Blackwell

Duncan, S. (1989) What is locality? in R. Peet and N. Thrift (Eds.) *New Models In Geography.* Vol.2. London: Unwin Hyman (pp.221-252)

Duncan, S. and Savage, M. (1991) New perspectives on the locality debate. *Environment and Planning A.,* 23, 2, 155-164

Duncan, S. (2002) *Space, Localities and Social Policy.* Unpublished paper. University of Bradford Department of Social Sciences and Humanities

Geddes, P. (1968) *Cities In Evolution. An introduction to the town planning movement and to the study of cities.* London: Ernest Benn (Original edition, 1915)

Giddens, A. (1984) *The Constitution Of Society.* Cambridge: Polity

Gillespie, R. (2002) Architecture and power: A family planning clinic as a case study. *Health & Place,* 8, 3, 211-220

Green, B. (1982) Structural antecedents of psychoactive drug use among the elderly. *Ageing and Society* 2, 1, 77-94

Halford, S. & Leonard, P. (2006) Place, space and time: contextualizing workplace subjectivities. *Organization Studies* 27, 5, 657-676

Healy, J., Victor, C., Thomas, A., and Seargeant, J. (2003) Professionals and post-hospital care for older people. *Journal of Interprofessional Care,* 16, 1, 19-29

Hurst, M.E.E. (1985) Geography has neither existence nor future. in R.J. Johnston (Ed.) *The Future of Geography* London. Methuen (pp.59-91)

Law, J. 2006. *Big Pharma. How the world's biggest drug companies control illness.* London. Constable

Lym, G. 1980. *A Psychology Of Building. How we shape and experience our structured spaces.* New Jersey. Prentice-Hall

Martin, G. and Wheeler, K. (Eds.) (1975) *Insights Into Environmental Education.*

Edinburgh: Oliver and Boyd

Massey, D. and Jess, P. (Eds.) (1995) *A Place In The World? Places, cultures and globalization.* Milton Keynes: The Open University

Oliver, M. and Sapey, B. (1999) *Social Work With Disabled People.* (2nd ed.) London: Macmillan

Paasi, A. (1991) Deconstructing regions: Notes on the scales of spatial life. *Environment and Planning A,* 23, 2, 239-256

Peet, R. and Thrift, N. (Eds.) (1989) *New Models in Geography.* Vol.2. London: Unwin Hyman

Phillipson, C. (2007) The 'elected' and the 'excluded': Sociological perspectives on the experience of place and community in old age. *Ageing and Society,* 27, 321-342

Phillipson, C. (1989) Developing a political economy of drugs and older people. *Ageing and Society,* 9, 4, 431-440

Plant, B. and McFeely, S. 2004. *Working With Young People: Real stuff.* Salisbury. AP

Popay, J., Thomas, C., Williams, G., Bennett, S., Gatrell, A., and Bostock, L. (2003) A proper place to live: Health inequalities, agency and the normative dimensions of space. *Social Science and Medicine,* 57, 55-69

Sommer, R. (1974) *Tight Spaces. Hard architecture and how to humanize it.* New Jersey: Prentice-Hall

Stea, D.(1976). *Environmental Mapping.* Milton Keynes: Open University Press

Urry, J. (1985) Social relations, space and time. in D. Gregory and J. Urry (Eds.) *Social relations and spatial structures.* Basingstoke: Macmillan

Ward, C.(ed).1973. *Vandalism.* London: The Architects' Press

Wilkinson, P. and Bissell, G. (2005) The 'Place' of placements. *Practice,* 17, 4, 285-298

Notes for contributors

The Journal of Practice Teaching in Health and Social Work covers all aspects of practice teaching (field education) and training and education in workplace settings. Articles may also consider the policy context of training and education and the impact of the changing expectations of service users and the public.

We welcome papers from any country in the world. Case studies, research reports, policy appraisals and narrative articles on the philosophical principals underlying this field of activity (practice teaching/field education) are equally acceptable. Material should be practically relevant to what trainers, managers and workers actually do. Articles should run between 2000 and 6000 words, with a preference for the shorter article.

Articles are sought from (among others): practice teachers and field educators; training staff and agency managers; teachers and researchers in higher and further education and policymakers with an involvement in this field. We are especially keen to encourage feedback from practising health and social work professionals and their managers on the effectiveness of existing training and education arrangements as preparation for work. We are therefore prepared to offer guidance to practice teachers and managers with staff development responsibility who do not publish regularly; as their contributions are likely to be of particular relevance.

The language of the journal is British English. Authors (including those from the UK!) should remember that even professional usage varies between regional forms of English and ensure terminology is comprehensible to those from other disciplines, countries and cultural backgrounds. In a multidisciplinary and international journal it may be necessary for authors to clarify local institutional and professional structures. We can give some assistance in respect on English idiom and expression to second language authors.

The journal will also carry: shorter pieces of up to 2000 words on some relevant topical issue; communications, rejoinders and letters; reviews of books, journals and training material and review articles; abstracts or listings of recent publications, conferences and relevant events.

Assessment for publication

When articles are received the editors make a decision on suitability for journal. Articles are sometimes rejected or returned to authors for major review at this stage. Otherwise, they are sent (anonymously) to two of the journal's advisors for assessment of their suitability for publication. The editors make the final decisions on publication, taking into account the views of the assessors, you will also receive personal feedback on the decision taken.

Presentation

Our preference is that articles should be submitted electronically as an email attachment in Word. If this is not possible, you should supply 4 copies of your paper with a summary of less than 150 words. On a separate cover sheet you should provide your name, address and professional details, together with telephone, fax and e-mail details. Where there are two or more authors, a single contact for correspondence and proofs should be indicated.

On acceptance for publication all references should be in the journal house style, the publishers can provide more detailed notes on the journal's format and style requirements.

You should indicate clearly how tables should be set out. For diagrams, charts etc, we will ask you to provide a final version meeting the journal's graphics guidelines. We do not provide an artwork service.

References

This journal uses the Harvard system of referencing. Authors must follow our house style for punctuation and use of upper and lower case letters and italics. Only works actually cited in the text in the text should be included in the references.

Copyright

You will be asked to assign copyright in your article to the journal. Consent for reproduction of your article in collections of your own work appearing subsequent to publication will be given without charge. You will receive two free copies of the journal upon application, and may order further copies at cost prior to the publication. Offprints are available at cost at anytime.

Editorial address

Steve Ambler, Deputy Editor, Papers, Journal of Practice Teaching in Health and Social Work, 7 Ermine Crescent, Stilton, Peterborough PE7 3RD. Steve@amblernet.com.

Call for papers

Themed issue: *Groupwork and older people*
Guest Editor: Professor Jonathan Parker

The world's population is ageing. This increases the need for opportunities to socialise, to develop a sense of community, continuity and enjoyment for many people. It also creates demands for older people to feel useful and to make a contribution to society. Importantly, our ageing societies result in greater numbers experiencing physical and mental health needs. Groupworkers have an especially valuable role in contributing to and enriching the lives of older people in a variety of settings and circumstances from providing support and information, facilitating member-led groups to therapeutic groups.

Are you a groupworker experienced in working with older people? The purpose of this special edition is to explore the creativity, value and significance of groupwork in working with older people. We would welcome theoretical papers, case studies and critical and reflective accounts of experiences in practice. Papers that address issues of cultural competence in groupwork with older people will be especially welcome. Professor Jonathan Parker has agreed to coordinate and edit this special issue.

If you would like to contribute or to discuss an idea, please let Jonathan Parker know as soon as possible. He would be very happy to discuss ideas for contributions in advance. Submissions will go through the journal's normal refereeing process. ***Please send proposals or contact Jonathan by 29 February 2008.***

Address and contact details for the Editor of this themed issue of *Groupwork*:

Professor Jonathan Parker
Bournemouth University, Royal London House, Christchurch Road, Bournemouth BH1 3LT, UK.
parkerj@bournemouth.ac.uk
Telephone: +44(0)1202 962810

Printed in the United Kingdom
by Lightning Source UK Ltd.
127198UK00001B/71-188/P